Don Troiani's Civil War
Cavalry & Artillery

Art by Don Troiani
Text by Earl J. Coates, Michael J. McAfee, and Don Troiani

STACKPOLE
BOOKS

Copyright © 2002 by Stackpole Books, Images © 2002 by Don Troiani
Introduction © 2006 by Stackpole Books

Published in paperback in 2006 by
STACKPOLE BOOKS
5067 Ritter Road
Mechanicsburg, PA 17055
www.stackpolebooks.com

Printed in China

10 9 8 7 6 5 4 3 2 1

FIRST EDITION

For free information about the artwork and limited edition prints of Don Troiani, contact:

Historical Art Prints
P.O. Box 660
Southbury, CT 06488
203-262-6560
www.historicalartprints.com

For information on licensing images in this book, visit www.historicalimagebank.com

Library of Congress Cataloging-in-Publication Data

Troiani, Don.
   [Don Troiani's regiments and uniforms of the Civil War. Selections]
   Don Troiani's Civil War cavalry and artillery / art by Don Troiani ; text by Earl J. Coates,
Michael J. McAfee, and Don Troiani.— 1st ed.
      p. cm.
   Reprints a section of the author's Don Troiani's regiments and uniforms of the Civil War.
Mechanicsburg, PA : Stackpole Books, c2002.
   ISBN-13: 978-0-8117-3317-5 (pbk.)
   ISBN-10: 0-8117-3317-3
   1. United States. Army. Cavalry—History—Civil War, 1861–1865—Pictorial works. 2. Confederate States of America. Army. Cavalry—Pictorial works. 3. United States. Army. Cavalry—Uniforms—History—19th century—Pictorial works. 4. Confederate States of America. Army. Cavalry—Uniforms—Pictorial works. 5. United States. Army. Artillery—Uniforms—History—19th century—Pictorial works. 6. Confederate States of America. Army—Artillery—Uniforms—Pictorial works. 7. Soldiers—United States—History—19th century—Pictorial works. 8. Soldiers—Confederate States of America—Pictorial works. 9. United States—History—Civil War, 1861–1865—Regimental histories. 10. United States—History—Civil War, 1861–1865—Pictorial works. I. Title: Civil War cavalry and artillery. II. Coates, Earl J. III. McAfee, Michael J. IV. Title.
E492.5.T76 2006
973.7'8—dc22
                                    2005027478

INTRODUCTION

THIS BOOK IS TAKEN FROM THE LARGER VOLUME *Don Troiani's Regiments and Uniforms of the Civil War* to provide a less expensive reference source for those interested in specific areas of Civil War uniforms. The subject of Civil War cavalry and artillery could not be comprehensively covered in a number of small volumes such as this, but this publication will provide a good overview.

The most dashing of all the services was the cavalry while the artillery was the king of the battlefield. Since much of their equipment was mounted, the dress of artillerymen usually resembled that of the cavalry, which was distinguished largely by colored trim and insignia. The study of these branches encompasses not only uniforms, but also the horse equipment and the other specialty equipage unique to these services. In the portrayals shown in this volume, I relied on the original artifacts whenever possible.

My longtime friends, Earl J. Coates and Michael J. McAfee, represent the pinnacle of their fields in research, and working with them has always been an enjoyable and enriching experience. Contributing authors Tom Arliskis and David M. Sullivan, also leaders in their areas of study, presented fresh information and ideas. Working with primary source materials, period photography, and original artifacts gave us the opportunity to explore the dress of many units from a multidimensional perspective. Equally important was the wise counsel offered by some of the great Civil War collectors and students of material culture: James C. Frasca, John Henry Kurtz, Paul Loane, Dean Nelson, Michael O'Donnell, and John Ockerbloom, among many others. Their decades of practical hands-on experience provided knowledge that cannot be "book learned."

Posing fully dressed models for all the studies in the book also opened the vista of seeing what some of this stuff really looked like on the soldier. Reading about it is one thing; seeing it is quite another.

As the main topic is uniforms, we have not explored firearms or edged weapons as they are exhaustively covered by many other books. We have touched on accoutrements but not in anything approaching complete coverage, selecting mostly items that augmented illustrated uniforms.

In researching the figure studies, the authors consulted every available source. Despite our more than a hundred years of combined study, we recognize that there's a good chance that another interesting nugget of new or conflicting data, perhaps from an unpublished account or collection, could surface after this book's publication. But that is the way of historical research and, indeed, one of the facets that makes it both frustrating and fascinating. To those who are disappointed that a favorite regiment has been left out, please forgive me, I'll try to get to it in the future!

Don Troiani
Southbury, Connecticut

ACKNOWLEDGMENTS

I DEDICATE THIS BOOK TO MY FATHER, DOMINICK H. Troiani (1916–2005), 258th Field Artillery, HQ Company, 95th Infantry Division, who served his country in France and Germany in 1944–45. His war stories got me interested in all this as a child. I also dedicate it to all the gallant servicemen and women who continue to defend our country on a daily basis.

I owe a debt of gratitude to my distinguished friends Earl J. Coates and Michael J. McAfee, two of the greatest gurus on the subject of Civil War uniforms, who graciously tolerated all my ceaseless questions and, as always, shared the fruits of a lifetime research with me. They are genuinely "national treasures." Particular thanks to contributing authors Tom Arliskis, who provided important primary information on Western units, and David Sullivan renowned authority on Civil War marines.

Special credit to renowned Civil War author-photographer Michael O'Donnell for taking many of the fine color photos of artifacts for this book, and to Tracy Studios of Southbury, Connecticut.

The following individuals and institutions also contributed to the creation of this book: Gil Barrett, Bruce Bazelon, Carl Borick, Robert Braun, William Brayton, Major William Brown, William L. Brown III, Christopher Bryant, Rene Chartrand, Charles Childs, Dr. Michael Cunningham, Ray Darida, Dr. David Evans, William Erquitt, Robin Ferit, James C. Frasca, Joseph Fulginiti, Fred Gaede, Holly Hage- man, Charles Harris, Randy Hackenburg, Gary Hendershott, Bruce Hermann, Steven Hill, Robert Hodge, Mark Jaeger, Les Jensen, James L. Kochan, Robert K. Krick, Michael Kramer, John Henry Kurtz, John P. Langellier, William Lazenby, Claude Levet, Paul C. Loane, Edward McGee, Bob McDonald, Steven McKinney, Howard M. Madaus, Michael P. Musick, Dean Nelson, Donna O'Brien, John Ockerbloom, Stephen Osmun, Col. J. Craig Nannos, Dean Nelson, Larry Page, Andrew Pells, Ron Palm, Nicholas Picerno, the late Brian Pohanka, Cricket Pohanka, Kenneth Powers, Shannon Pritchard, Pat Ricci, Steven Rogers, Nancy Dearing Rossbacher, A. H. Seibel Jr., Mark Sherman, Sam Small, Wes Small, James R. H. Spears, Steve Sylvia, Brendan Synonmon, William Synonmon, David Sullivan, Donald Tharpe, Mike Thorson, Warren Tice, Ken Turner, William A. Turner, Cole Unson, James Vance, Michael Vice, Gary Wilkensen, Don Williams, and Michael J. Winey.

The Booth Museum of Western Art, Cartersville, Georgia; Confederate Memorial Hall, New Orleans; Charleston Museum, Charleston, South Carolina; Connecticut Historical Society; Connecticut State Library; New York State Collection; Pamplin Historical Park and the National Museum of the Civil War Soldier; Middlesex County Historical Society; The Company of Military Historians; the Nelsonian Institute; *North South Trader* magazine; The Horse Soldier; The Union Drummer Boy; and the West Point Museum, United States Military Academy.

The Cavalry

RIOR TO THE OUTBREAK OF WAR, THE U.S. ARMY mounted force was composed of five regiments: two regiments of dragoons, one of mounted rifles, and two of cavalry. For the most part, these troopers were scattered over the Western frontier, dealing with the problems presented by a white population who wished to settle lands loosely held for centuries by the Native Americans. On August 10, 1861, the adjutant general's office issued General Orders No. 55, which, to the chagrin of the dragoons and rifles, did away with the separate divisions and designated all as cavalry.[1] Once the shooting started, most of the Regular enlisted men of these regiments remained loyal to the Union, but several key officers with cavalry experience elected to join the Confederate cause.[2] In fact, Company A, 1st Confederate Regular Cavalry, was made up of men who deserted from the U.S. Army as they were leaving the Department of Texas. In essence, however, both armies, starting the war with a limited number of men with real cavalry experience, soon found themselves overshadowed by the influx of volunteers with little or no training in mounted service beyond what some had gained in the militia. Nevertheless, the daring exploits of these volunteers, both Union and Confederate, would rival those of any cavalry the world had ever seen. Together these Americans would write a new chapter in the use of mounted troops in warfare.

The prewar uniform worn by the U.S. mounted regiments had been adopted in part in 1854, with changes in 1858 adding the final touches. The facings on these uniforms—orange for dragoons, green for mounted rifles, and

yellow for cavalry—were a point of honor that, at a glance, distinguished the service of the trooper. General Orders No. 55 added insult to injury by eliminating the orange and green. Both dragoons and mounted rifles resisted receiving new uniforms trimmed in cavalry yellow until necessity overcame pride. War would certainly make such concerns seem trivial, although it was noted by Theophilus F. Rodenbough, by the historian of the 2nd Dragoons, that the regiment was able to stretch out the change for nearly two years.[3]

In the Federal army, the uniforms for both Regulars and volunteers of cavalry were manufactured or purchased by the Quartermaster Department, operating from Philadelphia's Schuylkill Arsenal and new depots established to meet the emergency. The supply procedures, as well as the methods of procurement, were the same as for the other branches. For the Confederacy, the Richmond Depot and other facilities across the South met the needs of the Southern troopers. With identical sources of procurement and supply for the cavalry,

Prewar dress epaulets of Capt. Alfred Pleasonton of the 2nd U.S. Dragoons. In 1851, the branch color of the two regiments of dragoons was changed to orange, which is represented in the circlets bearing the numeral 2 shown here. WEST POINT MUSEUM.

infantry, and artillery, it is not surprising that their basic garments, such as shirts and other undergarments, were identical. The uniforms of the cavalry, although distinct in some details, did not differ greatly from those issued to the rest of the army. The greatest distinctions were the bright yellow trim, at first scorned by the old-line Regular dragoons and rifles, and the air of superiority that seemed to set the trooper apart from those who must campaign on foot.

HEADGEAR

Union

The Federal trooper was authorized two types of headgear, a hat and a forage cap, both originally adopted by the army in November 1858.[4] Except for the trim and insignia, both of these were identical to those issued to the infantry. The hat was looped up on the right side and held by a brass eagle; brass crossed sabers (for dragoons and cavalry) and the company letter along with the regimental number were worn on the front of the crown. The enlisted men of the mounted rifles wore only the company letter on the front of the hat. The ornamentation was completed by a worsted wool cord, with tassels, the color of the branch, around the base of the crown, and a black feather attached in front and lying around the side opposite the looped-up brim. The pattern 1858 forage cap was made of a dark blue cloth, with a welt around the crown the color of the arm of service and the company letter on the front.

Both of these hats remained in service throughout the Civil War. The most significant change was the elimination of the colored welt on the forage cap early in the war, an economic measure that eliminated the need to supply separate caps for each branch of service. Many Federal cavalry regiments received an initial issue of both types of headgear. As the war progressed, the type of issue headgear actually worn varied, depending on the wishes of the commanding officer.

Existing orders make it apparent that many enlisted men attempted to express their individuality by adopting hats of varying types and colors. This practice usually resulted in orders condemning the practice, although at any given time a Federal trooper may have been seen sporting a hat that set him apart from his comrades. Orders and circulars from various regimental order books show clearly that headgear certainly attracted the attention of those in command.[5]

Orders no. 20   H.Q. 1st Vt. Cavalry
                                Camp near Harrisonville, Va.
                                July 11, 1862
     Commanders of companies will see that the enlisted men of their companies wear the uniform cap, recently issued by the Quartermasters and will see that none of their men wear slouch or straw hats in the ranks.

Orders no. 28   H.Q. 6th U.S. Cavalry
                                Jan. 23, 1863
     The Commanding officer has noticed the irregular and unmilitary appearance of many of the men, an evil increased by their being permitted to wear felt and white hats and in fact whatever they choose—Hereafter every man will be required to wear the regulation uniform cap. They are on hand and can and must be drawn today.[6]

Regimental Order no. 18   H.Q. 9th New York
                                                    Cavalry
                    near Culpeper C.H. March 4, 1864
     After April 1, 1864 and during the summer months no Forage caps will be worn by any trooper of this command. The U.S. Army hat (black) will be the style until further orders.
                                By order of
                                Wm. Sackett
                                Col. Cmdg. 9th N.Y. Cav.

Officer's forage cap believed to have been worn by Col. William Stedman of the 6th Ohio Volunteer Cavalry. With richly embroidered crossed sabers surmounted by a silver bullion numeral 6, this cap is an excellent example of high-quality officers' field headgear. It bears the maker's imprint, "US Akron." JAMES C. FRASCA COLLECTION.

Model 1858 Federal cavalryman's uniform hat, marked in the crown "Manufactured by James H. Prentice, Brooklyn, New York," who contracted for 50,000 such hats in October 1861. It was worn by John W. McClain of the 6th Ohio Volunteer Cavalry. Misshapen, with its top field-crushed down and soldier-made ventilation holes punched through, it vividly illustrates how these hats often appeared in the field. JAMES C. FRASCA COLLECTION.

E. J. COATES AND F. C. GAEDE, COMPS., "U.S. ARMY QUARTERMASTER CONTRACTS, 1861–1865" (UNPUBLISHED MANUSCRIPT, 1993), 234.

Circular   H.Q. 1st N. J. Cavalry
                         Oct. 21, 1864

Notwithstanding the orders that have been issued the Maj. Commanding has noticed with astonishment and regret, that several of the 1st Sgts. of companies continue to appear in slouch, unsoldierly hats. Hereafter any such will be ordered off the Parade, and a second offense will be followed by a reduction to the ranks.

Regimental Order no. 93   1st Maryland Cavalry
                                  November 1864

. . . enlisted men found wearing a hat while on duty after he shall have been supplied with a cap . . . will be severely punished."

General Orders no. 37   H.Q. 3rd Michigan
                                   Cavalry
           Brownsville, Ark. Dec. 27, 1864

. . . The black felt hat issued by the Government will be worn without trimmings, the crown being folded in the "Continental Style." The forage cap may be worn as undress or on fatigue and stable duty.

Confederate

Confederate uniform regulations initially called for a gray forage cap with a band around the lower edge the color of the branch of service. This was changed in January 1862 to require the cap body itself to be the branch color, with a dark blue band.[7] Since Confederate regimental procurement records rarely give anything but the cost of caps issued, the number of regulation caps actually reaching the field is difficult to establish. Confederate troopers, unlike their Northern counterparts, received either caps or hats, but rarely both. Regimental records, particularly in the Army of Northern Virginia, clearly show a regular issue of military caps. Whereas hats also often appear on receipts for clothing, the number of caps in nearly all cases is greater. This fact is substantiated by a report from the manufacturing branch of the Richmond Clothing Depot. On March 31, 1864, Capt. O. F. Weisiger reported receiving 58,442 cap fronts from Maj. W. G. Ferguson, quartermaster.[8] These may have been the caps contracted for with the firm of Peter Tait of Ireland, who was to send in "50,000 caps ready cut (grey cloth) with peak" during the first three months of 1864.[9] Whatever the case, the combined manufacturing and issue records speak loudly that the typical Confederate trooper in the East, like his Yankee foe, was probably more often than not dressed in the military cap. Records of manufacture in the depots supplying the Confederate armies in the Western Theater of the war often list hats and caps under the same accounting, making it more difficult to determine the actual issue. The fact that caps were easier and cheaper to produce makes it likely that the issue of caps to the armies serving west of the Allegheny Mountains was a common occurrence.

With all of this said, the only factor that is impossible to analyze is the Confederate trooper himself. It is well known that Confederate enlisted men often obtained headgear from unorthodox sources. Since there seems to have been much less attention to what the Confederate cavalryman was wearing to cover his head than is evident in the Union army, the actual percentage of hats versus caps will remain unknown.

JACKETS, BLOUSES, AND APPENDAGES
Union

Most of the enlisted men serving in the Union cavalry received both a uniform jacket and a fatigue blouse. The blouse was identical in all respects to that issued to all other branches of the army. The jacket, with its twelve-button front and high-standing collar, was identical to that issued to the light artillery except for the color of trim, which was cavalry yellow. It was a common practice for cavalrymen to have their jackets altered to a closer, more tailored fit than the standard issue. This tailoring often included lowering the collar, removing the pillows (belt supports), and shortening the length. At some point, apparently beginning in early 1863, the practice of removing the yellow trim from the jacket became a fad in both the Eastern and Western Theaters. As the fad spread, so too did the negative responses from commanding officers.

Regimental Order no. 25   9th Michigan Cavalry
                            May 12, 1863
     The Commanding officer notices that it is becoming a general custom for the Non-Commissioned officers and privates to rip off the braid on their uniform jackets thereby defacing and otherwise mutilating them. Such practices are positively forbidden . . . officers will see that it is immediately replaced.

Special Order no. 65   H.Q. 9th Penn.
                             Veteran Cavalry
                             Whiteside, Tenn.
                             Oct. 11, 1864
     . . . No enlisted man will be allowed to disfigure his uniform jacket by tearing off the regulation stripes, and for such offense will be stopped one months pay and if a non-commissioned officer reduced to the ranks.

Department of W. Va.   H.Q. 2nd Brigade,
                             Cavalry Division
                     Martinsburg, March 23, 1864
     . . . The stripping of braid from the dress jacket . . . is expressly forbidden.

It is difficult to determine the extent to which the jacket was worn in the field. Along with the cap, it is evident that the wearing of the jacket by enlisted men while on campaign was often left to the discretion of those in command.

Circular   H.Q. 3rd Division
                  Warrenton Junction Aug. 1, 1863
     Brigade Commanders will see that their commands will be furnished with Blouses in place of Jackets.

                         By Order
                         G. A. Custer Cmd. Division[10]

Regimental Order no. 69   H.Q. 13th
                            New York Cavalry
                     Vienna, Va. Nov. 14, 1863
     Commanders will see that their men wear the blouse except on Dress Parade, Guard, Inspection and such occasions as may be proper when they shall wear the uniform jacket. The jacket when not worn must be folded and always kept in perfect repair.

Circular [extract]   H.Q. 1st Vermont Cavalry
                       May 2, 1864
     Sergeants and Corporals can if they desire, wear the uniform jacket. All others will wear the blouse.

General Orders no. 7   H.Q. Cavalry
[part]   Middle Military Division
                         Dec. 2, 1864
     The use of jackets and hats by the men will be at once discontinued and the Blouse and cap with cross sabres and the letter of the Company attached will be instituted.
     An immediate inspection will be made to ascertain the number of Blouses, caps, cross sabres and letters required by each regiment and the requisition for the same sent in and filled at once.
     Commanding officers will hereafter approve no requisition for jackets and hats and compel the men of their command to habitually wear the Blouses and Caps.

                         By Command
                         Bvt. Maj. Gen. Torbert[11]

Shoulder Scales

Federal cavalrymen were one of the major recipients of brass shoulder scales, which had been universally issued to the pre-war mounted regiments. The scales, when received, were worn generally on dress parade and were considered an unnecessary nuisance by most troopers.

Confederate

The jacket of the Confederate cavalryman was manufactured by the same depots that made the nine-button uniform jacket that became the unofficial standard for the Confederate army. As a general rule, the only difference was yellow trim, which could be found on many depot-manufactured jackets for cavalry at least until the last year of the war. In addition, many Confederate cavalry jackets used a brass button with the single letter "C" for cavalry. Unlike the Federal trooper, the Confederate did not have a choice between fatigue and dress coats. What he was issued was what he wore. With very few exceptions, Confederate regimental records show receipts for jackets. It is rare that color is mentioned; however, when prices per garment are noted, they often vary slightly. A requisition for the 1st Virginia Cavalry filled on December 31, 1862, shows receipt of five jackets costing $12 each and four jackets priced at $12.50. No explanation is given, but since 50 cents was a sum to be considered at the time, there was obviously some variation in quality.[12] A similar receipt for items received by Company D of the 12th Virginia Cavalry, dated August 31, 1863, shows an even wider disparity, listing sixteen jackets at $14 each and twenty-two jackets at $12. On several occasions, this same regiment did note the actual color of jackets received. On April 15, 1863, Company K received twenty English gray jackets at $12 each. The following summer, Company G received both black and gray jackets, with no price given.[13]

DESIGNATING INSIGNIA

Union

Regimental Designation

Cavalry designating insignia consisted of stamped brass crossed sabers, with each saber measuring $3\frac{3}{4}$ inches, crossed in the middle; the regimental number, also of stamped brass, $\frac{5}{8}$ inch in height; and the company letter, 1 inch long. These were originally designed to be placed on the cavalry hat, but during the war they were also universally worn on the top of the forage cap. The order issued to the 1st New Jersey Cavalry on November 29, 1864, was repeated in the order books of the majority of Federal cavalry regiments: "The attention of Company Commanders is again called to the manner in which the cap ornaments are placed on the cap. In all cases the sabres must be evenly adjusted[,] the Company letter above the sabres and the number of the regiment below."

Corps Badges

Although detachments were often assigned to infantry headquarters, the Federal cavalry functioned as a separate corps in both the Eastern and Western Theaters of the war. No badge was officially adopted, and no order has been found specifying that any badge be worn by either Eastern or Western

cavalry regiments. The badge represented on some cavalry monuments commemorating actions of the Army of the Potomac Cavalry was worn by only a few officers.

Chevrons

Chevrons to designate noncommissioned officer rank were the same configuration for cavalry as for infantry or artillery, but their color was yellow. Although army regulations called for the chevrons to be worn above the elbow on each sleeve of the jacket or blouse, numerous entries in regimental order books attest to the fact that sergeants and corporals were often negligent when it came to sewing them on. Several reasons may account for this, not the least of which is that they had to pay for them. It may also be that the bright yellow stripes of command offered an inviting target for enemy sharpshooters. Whatever the reason, orders are abundant instructing those who failed in this regard to adhere to regulations:

General Orders no. 11 [part]   H.Q. 2nd Penn.
Cavalry
Dec. 3rd, 1862
. . . Hereby all non-commissioned officers must wear the proper badge of rank at all times.

Special Orders no. 65   H.Q. 9th Penn.
Veteran Cavalry
Whiteside, Tenn. Oct. 11, 1864
All non-commissioned officers of this Regiment are hereby ordered to wear the stripes and chevrons belonging to their respective grades.

Orders no. 29   H.Q. 6th U.S. Cavalry
Feb. 2, 1865
Non-commissioned officers are again instructed to wear the chevrons of their rank according to Regulations.

TROUSERS

Union

The trousers for mounted men in the Federal army were, with only a few exceptions, made of sky blue kersey wool, with an extra layer of this material in the seat and legs as reinforcement. Noncommissioned officers were required to wear trouser stripes of a width appropriate to their rank: $1\frac{1}{2}$ inches for sergeants and $\frac{1}{2}$ inch for corporals. For the cavalry, these stripes were made of yellow worsted wool. Most regiments had a man with sewing ability designated as a tailor, who was paid a nominal sum by newly promoted noncommissioned officers to apply the stripes to the trousers.

Black woolen overcoat worn by Maj. Hugh Mortimer Nelson of the 6th Virginia Cavalry, C.S.A. This coat features a red lining on the cape and oddly enough is fitted with South Carolina and U.S. ordnance buttons. Nelson served as an aide-de-camp to General Ewell and died of disease a few months after the battle of Gaines' Mill in 1862. TROIANI COLLECTION.

Confederate

Confederate troopers were issued the same trousers as the other branches of service. Regulations called for sky blue, which made captured Federal trousers a legitimate part of the uniform. Regimental records indicate that, as with the jackets, the trousers varied in quality and color. This fact is made evident in the prices, charged for trousers, that appear on receipts. The 12th Virginia Cavalry, on requisitions received in 1863, listed pants at $8, $11, $12, and $12.25. The same regiment received and issued trousers of light blue, dark blue, and gray. It can be safely assumed that those described as gray ran the complete range of shades of that color.[14]

OVERCOATS AND PONCHOS
Union

For comfort in cold and inclement weather, the Federal cavalryman was issued both an overcoat, or greatcoat, of sky blue kersey wool and a poncho of rubberized canvas. Quartermaster regulations described the coat as double-breasted, with a collar that could be worn turned up or folded down. The cape was long, extending to the cuff of the sleeve. The coat differed from that issued to the infantry, in both the double-breasted cut and the long cape, which were designed to give the trooper protection. When not worn, the overcoat was rolled and strapped to the pommel of the saddle.

The poncho was similar to the rubber blanket issued to the infantry, but it had a cut in the center with a fold-over flap large enough for a man's head to pass through. This arrangement allowed the trooper to wear the poncho draped over his body as a shield from the rain. If conditions warranted, both the coat and poncho could be worn.

> Special Orders no. 5 [part]   H.Q. 9th New York
> Cavalry
> Acquia Church, Va.
> February 15, 1863
>
> Hereafter upon marches, drill or inspections, Commanders of Companies will be held accountable for the dress of their respective commands[;] they will also have the men dressed according to the state of the weather; clear, moderate the dress jacket will be worn, cold the greatcoat in addition and in inclement weather the ponchos over the greatcoat.
> By Order;
> S. Nichols, Maj. Commanding[15]

Confederate

Overcoats for Southern troopers varied in style, color, and material. Regulations called for an overcoat of gray wool cut in the same manner as that issued to the Federal army. Regimental clothing receipts show that the Confederate government made every effort to provide coats for its soldiers. The very best overcoats received by Confederate soldiers of any branch were those run through the Union naval blockade from England. Confederate prisoners observed in December 1863 by Frank Rauscher, a member of the 114th Pennsylvania Infantry, were wearing "overcoats . . . of much better material than our own. They were of English manufacture, a much darker blue than [ours]."[16] The Tait proposal given to the Confederate secretary of war in December 1863 called for 50,000 greatcoats of "stout grey cloth cut and ready for sewing" to be received from England in the first months 1864.[17]

Despite the chance for "friendly fire" incidents, the Confederate troopers did not hesitate to make full use of captured Federal overcoats. This at times worked to their advantage. On the morning of October 4, 1864, a member of Blazer's Scouts, a Federal independent mounted command, was riding alone near Cedar Creek, Virginia, when he was captured by five mounted men dressed in Federal overcoats who he had suspected were Rebels. His narrative of the event, which appeared in a veterans' newspaper, the *National Tribune,* on October 31, 1889, leaves no doubt that this was far from an unusual occurrence.

Confederate cavalry regimental clothing receipts also mention the issuance of ponchos to Southern cavalry. Since the practical design of the poncho leaves little room for variation, it can be assumed that these were similar to those issued to Federal troopers.

FOOTWEAR
Union
The Union cavalryman was invariably issued leather boots. These were of a standard pattern and varied little throughout the war. The leg of the boot was twelve inches high, and the top was wide enough to allow the trooper to tuck in his trousers. Orders relating to the trousers being worn inside or outside the boots generally are specific only for units on dress parade, dictating that the trousers then be worn outside the boot.

> General Orders no. 9 [part]   1st Brigade,
> 2nd Division
> Cavalry Corps, Army of the Potomac
> Oct. 18, 1864
> On all reviews and inspections or parades, unless in bad weather, trousers will be worn outside of the boots.
> By Command;
> Brig. Gen. Davies[18]

It can be presumed that on the march, the decision whether to tuck the trousers into the boots was left to the discretion of the individual trooper.

Confederate
The shortage of leather in the Confederacy made the issue of boots to the Confederate cavalryman anything but standard. Regimental records occasionally show boots but far more often show shoes being received by the Southern trooper. Regimental records of the 1st Virginia Cavalry show mixed issues of boots and shoes until March 1864, when Company K received thirty-nine pairs of shoes and five pairs of boots. Thereafter in this regiment, only shoes are shown as items of issue.[19] As an example of the situation faced by the Confederate soldier, on September 27, 1863, Company H of the 1st North Carolina Cavalry received six pairs of cloth shoes for issue.

2ND U.S. CAVALRY, BUGLER, 1861

In the early days of the war, the men who made up the few regiments of the Regular army were held in awe by the multitude of volunteers who filled the ranks of the U.S. Army. This was doubly true of the dragoons, who arrived in the East from posts in the Far West. Here were men who had served for years in such places as Texas, New Mexico, and California. They were the very embodiment of legends and stories that many young men who had grown up in the East had read and dreamed of.

The 2nd Dragoons joined the Army of the Potomac after service in Utah, New Mexico, and Kansas. The scattered companies arrived in Washington piecemeal, with Company

K first, in July 1861, followed over the next several months by the remaining companies with the exception of Companies C, I, and G, which did not join the regiment until November 1862.

During this period, a transformation took place that was to change both the uniform and the organization of the dragoons. On August 3, 1861, the entire U.S. mounted force was consolidated into a single corps. Until then, this force had consisted of three regiments of cavalry, one of mounted rifles, and two of dragoons. Now they would collectively be known as the 1st through the 6th U.S. Cavalry. For the dragoons, this was a demoralizing blow. Not only did they lose the proud

Double rich cavalry major's shoulder straps backed with yellow velvet. This set was worn by Maj. Edward H. Wright of the 3rd U.S. Cavalry, an aide-de-camp to Gen. George B. McClellan. TROIANI COLLECTION.

Federal cavalry musician's uniform jacket, trimmed with yellow worsted herringbone braid across the breast. As signals in the mounted services were given by bugle, it was important for officers to be able to distinguish the trumpeters in the smoke and excitement of conflict. Trumpeters generally rode gray horses to further visually set them apart from the rank and file. TROIANI COLLECTION.

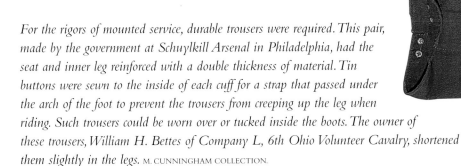

For the rigors of mounted service, durable trousers were required. This pair, made by the government at Schuylkill Arsenal in Philadelphia, had the seat and inner leg reinforced with a double thickness of material. Tin buttons were sewn to the inside of each cuff for a strap that passed under the arch of the foot to prevent the trousers from creeping up the leg when riding. Such trousers could be worn over or tucked inside the boots. The owner of these trousers, William H. Bettes of Company L, 6th Ohio Volunteer Cavalry, shortened them slightly in the legs. M. CUNNINGHAM COLLECTION.

title of "dragoon," but the color of their uniform trim would change from "the cherished orange . . . to the gaudy yellow" of the cavalry, as the historian of the 2nd Dragoons, Theophilus F. Rodenbough, put it. To lessen the impact, the original order allowed the dragoons to continue to wear the orange until their uniforms wore out and existing stocks of uniforms were exhausted. It was nearly two years before the last dragoon was forced by necessity to finally become amalgamated into the cavalry.

At this same time, another change in uniform that was much disliked by the Regulars was ordered. In December 1861, the secretary of war issued General Orders No. 101,

directing that the color of the trousers be changed from dark blue to sky blue. For many, this change was made only after the dark blue was no longer available. Consequently, some Regulars, despite the rigors of service in the field, managed to retain the dark blue as late as January 1863.

The 2nd Cavalry served with distinction throughout the Civil War as part of the Cavalry Corps of the Army of the Potomac. In 1865, as the volunteers returned home to a heroes' welcome, the men of the 2nd U.S. left camp in Maryland and proceeded to Fort Leavenworth, Kansas, and their old stamping grounds, the Plains.

The Bolivar Troop, Company A, 1st Battalion Mississippi Cavalry

The Bolivar Troop was recruited in Bolivar County, Mississippi, in late 1860 in response to Lincoln's victory in the presidential election of that year and the impending threat of war. Capt. Frank Armstrong Montgomery took great pride in the fact that his company was part of the independent Army of Mississippi. Mississippi seceded from the Union on January 9, 1861, and for a period of five weeks assumed the status of a sovereign nation, until becoming part of the Confederate States of America.

The "Ordinance to Regulate the Military System of the State of Mississippi" of January 23, 1861, called for ten cavalry companies to be organized. Under this ordinance, each

Bolivar Trooper was issued two Colt revolvers, a saber, and a Maynard carbine. Captain Montgomery noted in his memoirs, "My company for the time was very well-armed!" A private in the Noxubee Cavalry, which also served in Miller's Battalion, wrote that the weight of two pistols, saber, and carbine was so heavy that they had trouble mounting their horses. The pistols were afterward kept in holsters on the saddle horns.

Military equipment was scarce in Mississippi, so Captain Montgomery traveled through the South to procure provisions for his troop. While in New Orleans, he purchased for himself and his lieutenants new officers' sabers and belts,

Quilted jean cloth hat worn by Pvt. Landon Cheek of the 1st Mississippi Cavalry. Of particularly sturdy construction, the crown has small ventilation holes to allow air to circulate. CONFEDERATE MEMORIAL HALL, CLAUDE LEVET PHOTOGRAPH.

along with some "very handsome" cavalry saddles. Each trooper was to provide his own horse, and Montgomery found saddles for his enlisted men in Memphis. With great pride, he commented that by the time they left Memphis, they "made a very soldier-like appearance."

A description of 5th sergeant Frank A. Gayden, captured near Charleston, Missouri, in August 1861, provides some details about their uniform. Gayden, "greatly crestfallen at his capture," was dressed in a "gray shirt and had a broad yellow stripe on his pants. [He was] armed with a splendid Maynard rifle, a pair of Colt's Navy revolvers, and a cavalry sword."

The Bolivar Troop's uniform, though unique, generally followed the uniform prescribed under Mississippi's ordinance. General orders stated that each cavalryman was to wear "for fatigue . . . a blue flannel shirt with a star of white on each side of the collar." Trousers were to be "gray, with a stripe one inch wide, of the facings of their respective corps." For cavalry, the facings were yellow at first, and orange was added in May 1861. The men wore overshirts of light blue-gray, with all trim, including rank stripes, of a solid black. Their trousers were a shade of blue. The men wore hats of gray felt, pinned on the right side with a white metal star or button and a black ostrich plume, and adorned on the front with the brass letters "BT" in old script.

Captain Montgomery's overshirt was of a similar style but had large, dark, pointed cuffs, ornamented with two buttons. He wore the prescribed captain's shoulder straps of "dark blue cloth, bordered with an embroidery of gold, one quarter of an inch wide, with two embroidered bars" to denote his rank.

While at Union City, Tennessee, in June 1861, the battalion was formed from different Mississippi cavalry companies serving under Gen. Frank Cheatham of Tennessee. John Henry Miller of the Pontatoc Dragoons was elected major. The Bolivar Troop then became Company A of Miller's 1st Battalion of Mississippi Cavalry.

On April 2, 1862, just days before the battle of Shiloh, a consolidated regiment, the 1st Improvised Mississippi Cavalry, under Col. A. J. Lindsay, was formed. The Bolivar Troop became Company H of this new regiment. The regiment was reorganized at Tupelo, Mississippi, in May 1862, with the twelve-month men having now reenlisted for the duration of the war. Captain Montgomery was elected lieutenant colonel, and Capt. Richard A. Pinson was elected colonel of the Mississippi 1st Cavalry Regiment.

The soldiers of the Bolivar Troop finished the war in Gen. Frank C. Armstrong's Brigade, Chalmer's Division, Forrest's Cavalry Corps, Department of Alabama, Mississippi, and East Tennessee. Battle credits list over 100 engagements, skirmishes, or major battles—a proud military history for a "hell-roaring Battalion of Cavalry."

1ST NORTH CAROLINA CAVALRY, OCTOBER 1861

The 1st North Carolina Cavalry was raised in that state in the summer of 1861. They would serve, largely with the hard-fighting cavalry of the Army of Northern Virginia, until the final surrender at Appomattox. The regiment received its initial issue of uniforms and equipment from the state in early October. This uniform consisted of a sack coat of gray cloth from North Carolina mills. This same style was issued to nearly all early North Carolina units, with each branch of service distinguished by color of trim. Throughout the war, North Carolina made every effort to assure that her sons were well clothed and supplied. The distinctive cut of the initial issue changed from a coat to a jacket by the second major receipt of clothing in May 1862.

If the clothing issued in 1861 showed a great degree of uniformity, the Ordnance received by the 1st North Carolina did anything but. Although well armed, the Carolinians carried a diversity of weapons, including a variety of muzzle-loading pistols, revolvers, rifles, carbines, and sabers. One company received the artillery version of the Colt revolving carbine; however, by August 1862, most of these were listed as needing repair. As with the majority of Confederate cavalry regiments, this variety of arms did not improve, but the problem in fact became more pronounced as the war continued.

Included in the intriguing items of early issue to the regiment were a number of white buff saber belts, of Mexican War vintage. Also of particular interest were the saddles received. While some troopers rode on Texas Ranger–style saddles, others were issued saddles referred to as the New Orleans or Nashville style. No matter what arms or saddle they used, the troopers of the 1st North Carolina gave a good account of themselves in some of the hardest-fought cavalry battles ever waged.

MICHAEL FLANAGAN

Mounted Rifle Rangers, January 1862

In September 1861, Gen. Benjamin Butler was authorized to raise a division of troops in New England. Needing cavalry, Butler in turn authorized twenty-five-year-old S. Tyler Read of Attleboro, Massachusetts, to raise two companies and H. A. Durivage to raise one. These three unattached companies of Massachusetts cavalry would be the only mounted force in Butler's New Orleans expedition.

Read's companies were recruited as the Mounted Rifle Rangers, a name that no doubt brought visions of adventure and glory to the minds of young men, while Durivage's company was known as the Light Cavalry. The uniforms for the three companies reflected the nature of the service that their names implied. A reporter for the *Boston Evening Journal* was impressed by the sight of Captain Read's men: "They carry heavy sabres and short rifles, and are to be provided with revolvers beside. The uniform, without being showy, is a very superior and imposing feature of the equipments, and reflects great credit upon Pierce Bros. & Co., of this city, by whom it was manufactured. The overcoats are of dark blue cloth, the collars being trimmed with green cord. The jackets are trimmed with green, and the shoulders mounted with brass scales." The Rifle Rangers had also been issued headgear of a pattern patented in July 1861 by John F. Whipple of New York. The "short rifles" noted were Sharps carbines. The Rifle Rangers did not receive Colt army revolvers until June 1862, after the companies arrived in New Orleans.

In June 1863, the two companies of Rifle Rangers, as well as the Light Cavalry company, were assigned to the 3rd Massachusetts Cavalry, newly organized in Louisiana from the 41st Massachusetts Infantry. It is doubtful that Read's proud troopers were happy with this change. Early inspection reports of the foot soldiers-turned-cavalrymen were anything but favorable. Two months after formation, a colonel from the inspector general's office commented, "I consider this regiment in anything but effective condition, and as having few claims to the title of 'Cavalry.'"

U. S. CAVALRY MUSEUM, FORT RILEY, KANSAS

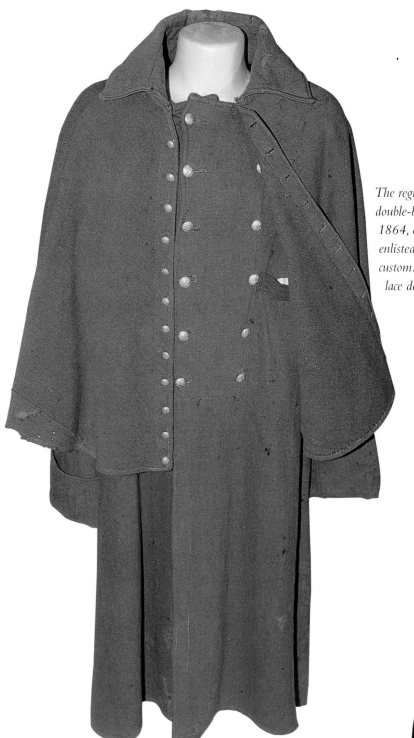

The regulation sky blue Kersey overcoats for mounted soldiers were double-breasted and had longer capes than those of foot troops. In 1864, officers were authorized to wear the same overcoat as the enlisted men, sanctioning what had in effect already been a popular custom. This coat was worn by a colonel, as indicated by the black lace denoting rank at the cuff. M. CUNNINGHAM COLLECTION.

Forage cap with insignia of Company F, 15th New York Volunteer Cavalry, used by Pvt. William H. Hosford, who carved his name and unit into the underside of the visor. Hosford died of disease in September 1864 at Cumberland, Maryland. TROIANI COLLECTION.

1st Arkansas Mounted Rifles, Private, Company D, 1861

The 1st Arkansas Mounted Rifles was raised at Little Rock in June 1861. Although the men were initially mounted, by April 1862 they had turned in their horses and would serve the rest of the war as infantry. As with most Trans-Mississippi Confederate volunteers, the initial procurement of both uniforms and arms for the regiment posed challenges that would have discouraged those of weaker will and determination. A September 25, 1861, letter from the quartermaster general's office in Richmond to the assistant quartermaster at Fort Smith, Arkansas, summed up the problem and said in part, "if you can procure any articles of clothing that are fit for issue to the troops you should do so. It is not pretended to supply a uniform, it cannot be done."

The early uniform of the 1st Arkansas is evidenced by issues shown in the clothing account book of Company D. Prior to early 1862, issues consist mainly of overshirts, pants, and shoes. This is clearly illustrated by an existing photograph of an officer of the regiment, that shows him uniformed in a manner that would have made him indistinguishable from an enlisted man. The clothing accounts of Company D show no issue of hats well into 1862, and it can be assumed that the men supplied their own. The hat shown is similar to many found on the steamboat *Arabia*, which was excavated near the present course of the Missouri River beginning in 1989.

As with most Trans-Mississippi regiments, the arms of the 1st Arkansas varied greatly. Regimental records show a quantity of Hall rifles being delivered in November 1861. These were most certainly part of the flintlocks taken from the Little Rock Arsenal.

After being dismounted in April 1862, the regiment moved east of the Mississippi and joined the Confederate Army of Tennessee. Their fate and future would be intertwined with that of this army until its surrender near Durham, North Carolina, on April 26, 1865.

DAVID RANKIN, JR.

6TH PENNSYLVANIA CAVALRY, 1861–65

With scarlet pennants fluttering from the ends of nine-foot lances made of Norway fir, the 6th Pennsylvania Cavalry, better known as Rush's Lancers, made a splendid spectacle on the parade ground. These antique weapons, however, were not found to be as practical on the many battlefields of the war as the twelve carbines initially issued to each company for picket and scout duty. Still, it was not until May 1863, more than a year and a half after the regiment's organization in Philadelphia by Col. Richard H. Rush, that the European-inspired lances were replaced entirely with carbines. By that time, Rush's Lancers had participated in the Peninsula campaign, Antietam, and Fredericksburg. They went on to fight in every major battle of the Army of the Potomac to Appomattox. Cavalry general John Buford praised the volunteers by dubbing them the "Seventh Regulars."

Despite their exotic weaponry, the uniforms of the 6th were basically those of all Union cavalrymen. Quartermaster General Montgomery C. Meigs wrote, "Colonel Richard H. Rush of Philadelphia[,] having authority from the War Department to such effect[,] you will furnish his Regiment of Cavalry . . . with the uniforms he desires, which I believe differs from the Regular uniform only in regard to trousers[,] they being light blue instead of dark blue." Some had their uniform jackets reworked by company tailors into nonstandard forms during the war, but in general, the men of the 6th looked like any Union cavalrymen without their lances.

1ST TROOP PHILADELPHIA CITY CAVALRY MUSEUM

8TH TEXAS CAVALRY, TERRY'S TEXAS RANGERS

Only a very few dedicated Civil War historians would immediately recognize the numerical designation of this famous regiment. But even the casual student would immediately be familiar with the name Terry's Texas Rangers. The regiment was originally raised in September 1861 to serve in Virginia but instead was diverted to service in the Western Theater of the war. It was here that Col. Benjamin F. Terry lost his life at the battle of Woodsonville, Kentucky, on December 17, 1861, and here that the regiment began to gain a reputation worthy of the Lone Star State.

As with most Confederate regiments, the uniform of the rangers varied during the war depending on the availability of material at any particular time. They were at times supplied with red-trimmed jackets and red shirts. Pride in their state often took the form of a handmade "Lone Star" affixed to the favored slouch hat. Like other Texas regiments, they received clothing supplied by their home state for most of the war.

If their uniform varied, so did their arms. Perhaps indicative of their background, the rangers were always well supplied with revolvers, often carrying more than one per man. Early in the war, the regiment was also armed with a short double-barrel shotgun. Some of these had a bar and ring attached identical to those common to carbines such as the Sharps. A listing of ammunition required by the regiment, dated May 13, 1862, bears testimony to the variety of arms found in their ranks:

20,160 cartridges for Navy six shooters
6,000 cartridges for Army six shooters
5,000 cartridges for shotguns
25,000 cartridges, buck and ball cal. .69
4,000 cartridges for Mississippi rifle
1,000 cartridges for Enfield rifle

Other requisitions dating as late as July 1864 show an even greater disparity in arms being carried, due largely to captures from the enemy. Of particular interest is a note found in the file of Sgt. Robert Burns, dated June 20, 1864, which states that at that time the rangers had sixty captured Spencer repeating rifles, but "the men [were] refraining from their further acquisition only because of the difficulty of procuring ammunition."

Terry's Texas Rangers continued to serve until the final days of the war.

BRANDY STATION REVIEW

June 8, 1863, was a day of glory. When it came to cavalry operations, the horsemen of the Army of Northern Virginia, under the leadership of dashing Gen. J. E. B. Stuart, were the unchallenged masters of the field. On this day, General Stuart accompanied the army commander, Gen. Robert E. Lee, on a grand review of his proud troopers. The anticipated summer campaign was beginning, and it had started well. The army had scored a decisive victory on the field of Chancellorsville, but this had been largely an infantry fight. Now the men of the cavalry were eager to once again challenge the Federal horsemen.

Over the winter, the cavalry had received regular replacements of needed uniform items. Jackets, caps, and trousers were often requested and listed as received on requisition forms. All ordnance, including arms, ammunition, and leather goods, had also been supplied. As the commanding officers galloped by, their appearance alone was enough to instill pride and confidence in both officers and men. Both generals, uniformed in regulation gray, were the epitome of the Confederate high command—Lee the picture of authority, and Stuart the image of the Southern cavalier. Lt. Louis R. Fortescue, a Union officer captured on July 5, met and vividly remembered Stuart: "His regulation grey uniform was profusely decorated with gold braid, and was topped with a broad-brimmed black felt hat, pinned up at the side with a star from which drooped an extravagantly large ostrich feather. On his left breast was a shield, about two inches in width, which held a chain attached to the handle of a small stiletto, the blade being passed through the button holes of his coat." At this moment, the Confederate cavalry had reached its zenith. In less than twenty-four hours, Yankee cavalry would challenge them on this very field and, with a newfound fury, fight the greatest cavalry engagement ever witnessed on American soil.

A fine-quality Confederate cavalry officer's frock coat worn by Capt. Thomas Pinckney of the 4th South Carolina Cavalry, probably in 1864–65. It is trimmed with light yellow piping, gold tape sleeve braids, and buttons with a "C" designating cavalry. Although regulations called for solid-colored collar and cuffs, many officers' coats were trimmed with less ostentatious piping.
COLLECTION OF THE CHARLESTON (SOUTH CAROLINA) MUSEUM.

Quantrill's Guerrillas

DAVID RANKIN, JR.

On October 5, 1863, some 300 to 500 splendidly mounted and heavily armed men rode south through Jasper County, Missouri. Some were clad in complete Federal blue uniforms, others in ordinary civilian garb, while many wore a peculiar kind of overshirt. A loose blouse that was cut low in the front, the slit narrowing to a point above the belt and ending in a ruffle or rosette, it was worn over a regular shirt and tie. It was usually made of homespun jean cloth of a brownish color, though some were a brilliant scarlet. It had huge pockets, one on each breast and one on each side below, like those in a coat. Many were finely embroidered or decorated with beads by wives or sweethearts; others were coarse and plain. This was the famous guerrilla shirt, and the riders were the band of Capt. William Clarke Quantrill, whom the Confederacy had officially made a captain of Partisan Rangers. He and his men had been declared outlaws by the Union forces, but to his supporters in Missouri, he was a dashing, free-spirited protector, an avenging angel.

Uniform jacket of the 15th Pennsylvania Cavalry, trimmed with orange cording. Originally raised in 1861 as an independent company called the Anderson Troop, after Gen. Robert Anderson of Fort Sumter fame, the 15th was later expanded into a full regimental establishment. TROIANI COLLECTION.

The guerrilla shirt adopted over time by Quantrill's men became a distinctive uniform of sorts. Some men wore them tucked neatly into their trousers; others let them fly loose in the wind. Baggy trousers tucked into high-topped boots, a broad leather belt bristling with revolvers, and a round-brimmed hat cocked at an angle adorned with a feather or metal star completed the costume. One eyewitness commented that "you could always tell a bushwhacker, because they wore feathers or bunches of ribbons, etc. in their hats."

On August 21, 1863, Quantrill's guerrilla band, led by some of his men dressed in Federal uniforms and flying the national colors, raided and sacked Lawrence, Kansas, a stronghold of Union support. Joseph Savage remembered seeing "what he thought were Union soldiers, in low-crowned, broad-brimmed hats, all alike, unshaven, stoop-shouldered, all without coats—nearly all wore red-flannel shirts, begrimed with camp grease and dirt. They had thrown away their coats, knowing they could get new ones in Lawrence." Many were tied to their saddles with straps to prevent them from falling off their horses when asleep. They were grimy and dirty from the long night's ride. Quantrill was said to have been dressed in a brown guerrilla shirt.

In four hours of murderous rampage and revenge, Quantrill's men left 180 men and boys dead in the streets, dragging some from their homes to be murdered in front of their families. They set the torch to much of the city, with 154 homes and businesses burned, the loss estimated at over $1 million. It was Quantrill's belief that it was a bushwhacker's war of no surrender and no quarter on both sides.

The Lawrence massacre led to swift retribution, as Federal forces under General Orders No. 11 drove the residents of four Missouri border counties onto the open prairie, while Jayhawkers pillaged and burned everything left behind. Quantrill and his raiders participated in the Confederate retaliation for this atrocity. Colorfully dressed and well armed, usually with two navy six-shot Colt revolvers, and two or three more on the saddle, as well as a Sharps carbine or shotgun, they were a formidable foe to the Federal soldiers in Missouri. But when Union forces drove the Confederates back, Quantrill fled to Texas. His guerrilla band split into several smaller units, including one headed by his notorious lieutenant, "Bloody Bill" Anderson, known for wearing a necklace of Yankee scalps into battle. Quantrill was eventually killed while on a raid into Kentucky in 1865.

Even in Quantrill's death, he and his followers remained folk heroes to their supporters in Missouri. Several ex-raiders—the brothers Frank and Jesse James and Cole and Jim Younger—went on to achieve their own notoriety in the late 1860s by applying Quantrill's hit-and-run tactics to bank and train robberies.

Quantrill and his guerrilla raiders were at times horribly cruel and merciless to their enemies, soldiers and civilian alike. Even to other Confederates, they remained an enigma. Protectors of freedom or outlaws, Quantrill and his men wrote their own page in the history of the American Civil War.

TROOPER, 7TH VIRGINIA CAVALRY, 1863

Regulation kepi for cavalry officers worn by Capt. Julian G. Pratt of the 18th Virginia Cavalry. The elegant cap body of yellow wool (slightly faded) is bedecked with a gold lace quatrefoil on the crown and is finished off with a humble oilcloth visor. Pratt had three horses shot from underneath him at the third battle of Winchester, on September 19, 1864. GARY HENDERSHOTT.

As part of the illustrious Laurel Brigade, the 7th Virginia Cavalry helped create the legend of invincibility that surrounded the cavalry of the Army of Northern Virginia during the first two years of the war. Although raised primarily in the Shenandoah Valley, the regiment also included a number of Maryland men who left their native state to fight for the Southern cause. The 7th Virginia's battle record was second to none, with Brandy Station, Gettysburg, Ream's Station, and Cedar Creek among the many engagements it was involved in, but its greatest claim to fame was the fact that it was commanded by the dashing and legendary Turner Ashby. Although Ashby commanded the 7th for only a short time before his promotion to brigadier and subsequent death in a rearguard action near Harrisonburg, Virginia, the regiment was often referred to as Ashby's Cavalry.

The uniform and equipment of the 7th Virginia was typical of the cavalry of the Army of Northern Virginia. By the later months of 1862, overcoats and other items of clothing, arms, and equipment of British origin were making their appearance in the ranks of the Confederate army. In addition, Confederate arms-making facilities had begun to approach their full potential. On March 13, 1863, the 7th received the first of a number of Confederate-made Robinson carbines that would be issued to them. These carbines, manufactured in Richmond, were direct copies of the renowned Sharps carbines and rifles, but they were plagued with problems and often had to be turned in for repair.

Capt. Julian G. Pratt's frock coat is piped in yellow and has regulation rank insignia, but lacks the authorized solid yellow collar and cuffs. Plain officers' coats without facings were commonplace in the Confederate army. GARY HENDERSHOTT.

2ND MISSOURI CAVALRY, MERRILL'S HORSE

It is doubtful that any volunteer cavalry regiment had a more competent commanding officer than the 2nd Missouri Cavalry did in Col. Lewis Merrill. He had been appointed to command by Gen. John C. Frémont and the regiment was dubbed Merrill's Horse. Merrill had been a captain in the 2nd U.S. Cavalry and had extensive experience on the prewar frontier. He knew well how to train a cavalry regiment and how to instill both pride and efficiency in his men. One method was to adopt a distinctive uniform, and to strictly enforce how it was worn and maintained.

The uniform included a jacket trimmed in the regulation yellow, but with a distinctive pattern on its paneled front, and a sky blue forage cap with an orange welt around the crown as a tribute to Merrill's service in the 2nd Dragoons. "All additions to or alterations of this uniform as prescribed are positively prohibited," Merrill ordered, "and will not be tolerated under any circumstances." Early armament of the regiment included an M1843 Hall carbine, an M1860 Colt army revolver, and an 1840-pattern saber.

The service of the 2nd Missouri was hard and dirty, and lacked the glory of the cavalry that served with the major armies east of the Mississippi River. The regiment spent most of its existence fighting guerrillas in Missouri and Arkansas. To the troopers' credit, they did it well. Merrill remained in command of the 2nd until the end of the war. He continued to serve in the U.S. Army until his retirement in 1886. A part of this service included the destruction of the Ku Klux Klan in various parts of the postwar South.

EARL J. COATES

Medium blue forage cap worn by Pvt. Darius Seely of Company H, 2nd Missouri Cavalry, Merrill's Horse. Manufactured expressly for all the enlisted men of Merrill's command, this cap of officers'-quality materials has a distinguishing orange welt around the crown. Seely served throughout the war and prided himself on being a proficient forager and skirmisher.

TROIANI COLLECTION.

RANGER MOSBY

MICHAEL FLANAGAN

John Singleton Mosby and his command wrote a chapter in Civil War history that is as fascinating to historians today as it was to those young men who chose to follow him. Operating behind Union lines in Northern Virginia, he and his men employed tactics that caused much larger numbers of Federal troops to be diverted to protect vital supply lines.

Although small in stature, Mosby looked every inch the cavalier. Photographic records and published recollections never fail to show or mention the ostrich-plumed hat worn by Mosby and many of his command. Even when dressed in an officer's sack coat with a lieutenant colonel's rank on the lay-back collar, instead of the short double-breasted jacket he often wore, Mosby's bearing left no doubt as to his ability to command.

TROOPER, 12TH VIRGINIA CAVALRY, 1864

As part of the famed Laurel Brigade, the 12th Virginia Cavalry saw more than its share of war. The men who rode in the ranks of the regiment had been recruited in Virginia's Shenandoah Valley. For them, much of the war took on special meaning, as they were not only fighting for the Confederacy, but also defending the Valley, their home.

As with most Confederate regiments, the 12th received a variety of uniform pieces during the war. Although the gen-eral style of uniform remained constant, the material from which the various parts of the regimental garb were made varied greatly. As a result, the color and quality of the items were never consistent, as evidenced in the regimental person-nel files. On June 6, 1864, Company F received "25 pairs of trousers of which 14 were gray, 7 light blue and 4 dark blue. Also received were 26 Jackets, 14 gray and 12 black."

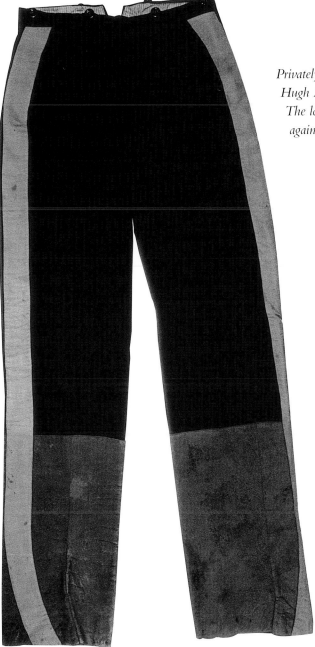

Privately purchased royal blue woolen trousers with wide yellow stripe, worn by Maj. Hugh Mortimer Nelson of the 6th Virginia Cavalry until his death in late 1862. The lower sections of the leg are sheathed in leather to protect the trouser bottoms against wear, a common practice for mounted troops. TROIANI COLLECTION.

Tall Confederate officer's forage cap, worn by Maj. Hugh Mortimer Nelson of the 6th Virginia Cavalry between 1861 and 1862. Maj. Gen. Thomas J. "Stonewall" Jackson wore a cap virtually identical to this one, complete with the civilian small brass flower buttons. TROIANI COLLECTION.

Other companies received similar assortments. Also prevalent was a mixed issue of headgear, which on occasion included a few "military caps." And though it may seem strange, by far the largest issue of footwear was not boots, but shoes.

Ordnance returns in various officers' files show a wide variety of arms used by the regiment, with several different makes and calibers of both carbines and revolvers often used within the same company. The regimental ordnance return for March 31, 1863, lists ammunition received for Enfield rifles, Colt army and navy revolvers, Colt revolving rifles, Sharps, Robinson, Merrill, and Smiths carbines. Later, a number of English Kerr revolvers were added, as well as other arms that the fortunes of war brought their way.

GEN. NATHAN BEDFORD FORREST

Confederate cavalry gained a solid reputation as an efficient and hard-fighting body in both the Eastern and Western Theaters of the war. In the West, such leaders as Gen. Nathan Bedford Forrest became famous for hard-hitting tactics that often led to victory over superior Union commands. From the beginning, the soldiers under Forrest's command were armed with a wide variety of sidearms, which included everything from shotguns to Colt revolvers. Uniforms also showed a wide diversity in style and color.

By mid-1863, Confederate clothing manufacture had reached a high degree of efficiency. Western commands such as Forrest's received much of their clothing from the facilities at Atlanta, Augusta, and Columbus, Georgia, as well as factories in such places as Montgomery, Alabama. Because these facilities received cloth from a number of diverse sources, uniforms were made in a variety of hues ranging from dark gray to shades of brown. Overcoats manufactured and supplied to Confederate forces were similar in cut to those worn by Union troops, but they generally had large, plain buttons in a variety of materials and colors. For the men who rode with Forrest, numerous encounters with their Federal opponents often supplemented the supply of uniforms they received from the South.

*Tan British Army–
issue saddle blanket
bearing a black,
stenciled, "broad
arrow" and "WD"
(War Department) marking. Capt. Charles S. Hill, ordnance officer of Gen.
Patrick Cleburne's division, wrote in December 1863, "I call to your attention
the frequent application made on me by both Field and Staff officers of this
Division for English saddle blankets & such necessities for officers. . . .
I understand there is a large quantity at Atlanta."* TROIANI COLLECTION.

One of Forrest's Men, First Sergeant, Rucker's Cavalry Brigade, July 1864

Gen. Nathan Beford Forrest was considered one of the finest cavalry generals to emerge from the war. His energy and spirit carried over to the men who rode and fought under his command. Forrest's men received uniforms from the various depots that supplied the Confederate Western armies. By 1864, most jackets produced in these depots no longer had the colored trim that indicated branch of service. Though many of these depots continued to supply forage caps, many, if not most, of the troopers preferred hats.

As with most Confederate cavalry, the arms carried by Rucker's Brigade included a mixed bag of muskets, rifles, carbines, and revolvers, though an inspection report for July 1864 shows that the brigade had no sabers. It was not uncommon for Confederate troopers to arm themselves with two revolvers.

There were many problems with the quality of saddles produced in Southern arsenals, and Yankee saddles of the McClellan pattern were prized items. A complaint from the ordnance officer of Wheeler's Cavalry Corps to the Atlanta Arsenal, referring to Confederate-made saddles, stated that "[t]he men in some cases refuse to take them, knowing that in most instances that they will last but a month or so and are certain to cause a sore back in a week or ten days." The sergeant shown here has reached beyond the normal Confederate supply system and recently acquired a new saddle compliments of Uncle Sam, complete with all the equipment of some hapless Union trooper.

ALEX DeQUESADA

Small, silver star badge lost on the battlefield of Utoy Creek, Georgia, on August 6, 1864, by an unknown soldier from the 3rd Texas Cavalry of Gen. Sol Ross's Brigade. Star emblems were favored by many other states in addition to Texas, including Mississippi and North Carolina. WILLIAM ERQUITT COLLECTION.

3RD NEW JERSEY CAVALRY, 1ST U.S. HUSSARS, 1864–65

Nicknamed the Butterflies because of their gaudy hussar-style uniforms, the 3rd New Jersey Volunteer Cavalry was not a bandbox regiment. The 3rd was recruited in the winter of 1863–64, and special permission was granted for the regiment's distinctive dress as a means of encouraging recruiting, even though it cost about $3 more per uniform than the regulation Federal-pattern cavalry uniform. At the regimental headquarters near Trenton, recruits poured in from January to March 1864, and by April, the regiment was completely equipped and mounted. It went immediately to Washington, where it joined the Army of the Potomac.

The Butterflies' uniform included a dark blue jacket with yellow cords across the breast and on the front of the orange collar, sky blue trousers with yellow stripes, a visorless cap that was worn tilted to the left, and a yellow-lined sky blue talma, or cloak. Although their colonel, Andrew Morrison, wanted only

D. Troiani © 93

sabers, the regiment was armed initially with three types of breech-loading carbines and Whitney and Colt revolvers. In November 1864, the regiment received Spencer repeating carbines, which the men put to good use. The 3rd served in such major battles as Winchester, Cedar Creek, Five Forks, Saylor's Creek and Appomattox. Mustered out in June 1865, the regiment had lost fifty officers and men in combat.

The uniform jacket owned by this sergeant of the 11th New York Cavalry, Scott's 900, was privately purchased and made of officers'-quality broadcloth with many elegant niceties lacking in the standard-issue garment. When this regiment was originally formed in early 1862, it was issued dark blue trousers. TROIANI COLLECTION.

4TH TENNESSEE CAVALRY, BLACK TROOPER, CHICKAMAUGA, SEPTEMBER 1863

By late 1863, the U.S. Army had realized the value and fighting potential of the black man. Throughout that year, numerous regiments of African-Americans had enlisted and seen action. For the Confederate army, however, it was not until the closing days of the conflict that the government formally sanctioned the enlistment of former slaves to fight for the South. Although numerous proposals were received from Confederate officers to organize black regiments, they all came too late. How many black men would have enlisted to fight for the South will always be a matter of speculation. That some would have willingly joined, however, is certain. From the beginning of the conflict, some had followed their masters into Confederate service as noncombatants in the same servile capacity they had fulfilled in civilian life.

As servants, the men remained behind the battle line and had ample opportunity to equip themselves with gear from casualties and prisoners. The result was that these men were often better equipped than the Confederate soldiers.

At the battle of Chickamauga, the servant of the regimental commander of the 4th Tennessee Cavalry proved that, like the man he served, he too was a leader of men. Having organized the other regimental servants into a "company" of about forty men, he demanded the right to follow the regiment into battle. First detailed to hold the horses of the white soldiers, the black company moved forward to the battle line and plunged into the fight along with the regiment, suffering four killed and seven wounded. The informal organization of this "company" of black Confederates left no record of their uniform, equipment, or arms.

The trooper shown here is largely outfitted with pieces of Union uniforms that had come his way during the months of campaigning with his master's regiment. A Union forage cap, Union mounted trousers, and boots taken from some

WILLIAM GLADSTONE

unfortunate Federal trooper are worn along with a Confederate infantry jacket of the style worn by Kentucky's famed Orphan Brigade. The vest may have been given the trooper by the officer he served. The checked shirt is of a style issued in large quantity to the Army of Tennessee. He carries a Federal-issue infantry overcoat and wears Federal accoutrements that were found in abundance on many battlefields. His arms, a Colt navy revolver and a Sharps carbine, were recent finds.

Sources

The Cavalry

INTRODUCTION

1. National Archives, Record Group 94, entry 44, Adjutant General's Office Orders and Circulars.
2. Ibid., Record Group 109, Compiled Service Records of Confederate General and Staff Officers, file of Capt. John Bradley.
3. Theophilus F. Rodenbough, comp., *From Everglade to Canon with the Second Dragoons* (New York: D. Van Nostrand, 1875).
4. National Archives, Record Group 92, entry 2182, War Department General Orders no. 13, November 13, 1858.
5. Ibid., Record Group 94, Regimental Books.
6. Ibid., Record Group 391, entry 821, Orders from August 1861 to February 23, 1863.
7. Ibid., Record Group 109, chapter 1, Adjutant and Inspector General, vol. 202.
8. Ibid., M-331, Compiled Service Records of Confederate General and Staff Officers.
9. Ibid., M-437, Letters Received by the Confederate Secretary of War.
10. Ibid., Record Group 393, entry 1449, Orders, 3rd Division Cavalry Corps, Army of the Potomac.
11. Ibid., Record Group 94, Regimental Order Books, 8th New York Cavalry.
12. Ibid., Record Group 109, M-324, Compiled Service Records of Confederate Soldiers from the State of Virginia, 1st Virginia Cavalry.
13. Ibid., 12th Virginia Cavalry.
14. Ibid.
15. Ibid., Record Group 94, Regimental Books, 9th New York Cavalry.
16. Frank Rauscher, *Music on the March, 1862–65: With the Army of the Potomac, 114th Regt. P. V. Collis Zouaves* (Philadelphia: Wm. F. Bell, 1892), 134.
17. National Archives, Record Group 109, M-437, Letters Received by the Confederate Secretary of War.
18. Ibid., Record Group 94, Regimental Books, 1st Pennsylvania Cavalry.
19. Ibid., Record Group 109, M-324, Compiled Service Records of Confederate Soldiers from the State of Virginia, 1st Virginia Cavalry.

2ND U.S. CAVALRY, BUGLER, 1861

Theophilus F. Rodenbough, *From Everglade to Canon with the Second Dragoons* (New York: D. Van Nostrand, 1875).
National Archives, Record Group 92, entry 2182, box 17, T. T. S. Laidley to Dept. Q.M. General Geo. H. Crosman, January 27, 1863.

THE BOLIVAR TROOP, COMPANY A, 1ST BATTALION MISSISSIPPI CAVALRY

Frank Alexander Montgomery, *Reminiscences of a Mississippian in Peace and War* (Cincinnati: Robert Clarke Company, 1901), 39, 44.
J. C. Deupree, *The Noxubee Squadron of the First Mississippi Cavalry, C.S.A., 1861–1865,* Mississippi Historical Society Publications 2 (1899): 15.
St. Louis Democract, August 16, 1861.
"Orders of the Military Board," in *Southern Military Manual* (Jackson, Miss.: J. L. Power, 1861), 7, 9.
Photographs, Herb Peck Collection.

1ST NORTH CAROLINA CAVALRY, OCTOBER 1861

Frederick P. Todd, *American Military Equipage, 1851–1872* (n.p.: Chatham Square, 1983), 2: 1060.
National Archives, Record Group 109, M-270, Compiled Service Records of Confederate Soldiers Who Served in Organizations from the State of North Carolina, Records of 1st North Carolina Cavalry; files of Capt. George W. Folk; Ordnance Sgt. Wm. D. Anthony, and Col. William C. Cheek.

MOUNTED RIFLE RANGERS, JANUARY 1862

Rev. James K. Ewer, *Third Massachusetts Cavalry, Company C,* Historical Commission of the Regimental Association, (Maplewood, Mass.: William G. J. Perry Press, 1903), 277–82.
Boston Evening Journal, December 31, 1861.
National Archives, Record Group 94, Regimental Papers, 3rd Massachusetts Cavalry.

1ST ARKANSAS MOUNTED RIFLES, PRIVATE, COMPANY D, 1861

James L. Nichols, *The Confederate Quartermaster in the Trans-Mississippi* (Austin: University of Texas, 1964).
National Archives, M-900, roll 1, Confederate Quartermaster General Letters and Telegrams Sent; Record Group 109, chap. 8, vol. 45.

Ron Field, *Brassey's History of Uniforms: American Civil War, Confederate Army* (Herndon, Va.: Brassey's, 1998), 82.

Steamboat *Arabia* Museum, Kansas City, Missouri.

National Archives, M-376, Compiled Service Records of Confederate Soldiers, Arkansas.

Peter A. Schmidt, *Hall's Military Breechloaders* (Lincoln, R.I.: Andrew Mowbray Publishers, 1996), 121.

6TH PENNSYLVANIA CAVALRY, 1861–65

Samuel P. Bates, *History of the Pennsylvania Volunteers* (Philadelphia, 1868), 741–753.

National Archives, Quartermaster Group, Clothing Series, Letter Book 18.

8TH TEXAS CAVALRY, TERRY'S TEXAS RANGERS

Frederick P. Todd, *American Military Equipage, 1851–1872* (n.p.: Chatham Square, 1983), 2:1218.

Correspondence with Norm Flayderman, who has a similar 8th Texas shotgun in his collection.

National Archives, Record Group 109, M-323, Compiled Service Records of Confederate Soldier Who Served from the State of Texas, file of John A. Warton, Colonel 8th Texas Cavalry.

BRANDY STATION REVIEW

National Archives Record Group 109, Compiled Service Records of Various Confederate Cavalry Commands.

Diary of Lt. Louis R. Fortescue, attached to the U.S. Signal Corps, captured on the Confederate retreat from Gettysburg, War Library and Museum, Military Order of the Loyal Legion of the United States, copy in Brake Collection, U.S. Military History Institute.

QUANTRILL'S GUERRILLAS

William Elsey, *Quantrill and the Border Wars* (New York: Connelly Pageant Book Co., 1909), 215, 317, 318, 347, 362.

TROOPER, 7TH VIRGINIA CAVALRY, 1863

Richard L. Armstrong, *7th Virginia Cavalry,* Virginia Regimental History Series.

National Archives, Record Group 109, M-324, roll 177, Regimental Personnel files of the 7th Virginia Cavalry, file of Lieutenant Colonel Marshall.

John M. Murphy and Howard M. Madaus, *Confederate Rifles and Muskets* (Newport Beach, Calif.: Graphic Publishers, 1996).

2ND MISSOURI CAVALRY, MERRILL'S HORSE

Francis B. Heitman, *Historical Register and Dictionary of the United States Army* (Washington, D.C.: Government Printing Office, 1903).

National Archives, Record Group 94, Regimental Books, 2nd Missouri Cavalry, Personal Service Record, Lewis Merrill; Record Group 156, Quarterly Ordnance Returns.

RANGER MOSBY

National Historical Society, *The Image of War, 1861–1865* (Garden City, N.Y.: Doubleday & Co., 1983), 4:141–42.

TROOPER, 12TH VIRGINIA CAVALRY, 1864

National Archives, Record Group 109, M-324, Compiled Service Records of Confederate Soldiers Who Served in Organizations from the State of Virginia, Records of the 12th Virginia Cavalry.

GEN. NATHAN BEDFORD FORREST

National Archives, Record Group 109, M-935, Monthly Inspection Report, Wheeler's Cavalry Corps.

ONE OF FORREST'S MEN, FIRST SERGEANT, RUCKER'S CAVALRY BRIGADE, JULY 1864

National Archives, Record Group 109, M-935, Monthly Inspection Report, 6th Brigade, 1st Division, Wheeler's Cavalry Corps, June 1864; M-331, file of Lt. Col. Moses H. Wright, Ordnance Officer, Atlanta Arsenal; file of Capt. S. P. Kerr, Ordnance Officer, Wheeler's Corps, from Tunnel Hill, Georgia, April 20, 1864.

3RD NEW JERSEY CAVALRY, 1ST U.S. HUSSARS, 1864–65

Michael J. McAfee, "3rd Regiment New Jersey Volunteer Cavalry, 1864–65," *Military Images* 21, no. 4 (January–February 2000): 6–7.

John Elting and Roger Sturcke, "1st U.S. Hussar Regiment, 1864–1865," *Military Collector and Historian* 30, no. 1 (spring 1978): 13–16.

4TH TENNESSEE CAVALRY, BLACK TROOPER, CHICKAMAUGA, SEPTEMBER 1863

National Archives, Record Group 109, M-251, file of A. I. Peeler, Company I, 5th Florida Infantry; M-275, Records of General and Staff Officers and Nonregimental Enlisted Men, file of Capt. C. L. Moore.

Charles Kelly Barrow, J. H. Segars, and R. B. Rosenburg, *Forgotten Confederates: An Anthology About Black Southerners,* Journal of Confederate History Series, vol. 14 (Atlanta: Southern Heritage Press, 1996), in the *Hawkinsville Georgia Dispatch,* February 5, 1885.

The Artillery

DURING THE CIVIL WAR, ARTILLERY PLAYED A SIG–nificant role in every major battle. Unlike the other combat arms, however, artillery never acted alone. Placed in its proper perspective, artillery is an important, and potentially decisive, supporting arm for both infantry and cavalry. This fact was recognized by Antoine Henri Jomini in his classic work *The Art of War,* first published in 1838, which was widely studied by Civil War officers. Jomini stated that it was "not right to say that artillery can act independently of the other arms, for it is rather an accessory."[1]

For centuries, artillery has been divided into two distinct types, heavy and light. The designation was decided by the size of guns the artillery served, which determined the role it would play in any military action. In simplest terms, heavy guns were generally confined to fortifications, whereas light guns accompanied the army into the field. The light artillery could be mounted or on foot, depending on whether it was being used in support of infantry or cavalry.

Uniforms for both the Union and Confederate artillery were manufactured and issued in the same manner as those for the cavalry and infantry. In many cases, the uniform items issued depended on the type of service to be performed by the soldier. In the North, the major depots, located in Philadelphia, New York, Cincinnati, and St. Louis, procured or manufactured most of the uniforms for the artillery. Southern artillery uniforms were obtained from the various established depots scattered from Virginia to Texas. A look at the clothing worn by the cannoneers of both armies will show the differences that distinguished Yankee from Rebel, as well as the variations that set the artillery apart from the other branches of service.

HEAVY ARTILLERY

UNION

The heavy artillery served guns that were, in general, too large to be taken into the field. Because they were usually confined to fortifications, which potentially could be over-run by enemy infantry, heavy artillery soldiers spent a good deal of time drilling as infantry, preparing to fight the invaders on their own terms. The service required of these soldiers dictated that the uniform they wore be nearly identical to that of the infantry.

Headgear

Initially many heavy artillery enlisted men were from the Regular army and, as prescribed by army regulations, had received both the M1858 dress hat and the forage cap. As the system of earthwork forts was built to protect Washington and other cities liable to Confederate attack, large numbers of volunteers were pressed into service to man them. Many of these volunteers had enlisted to serve as infantry but now found their regiments converted to heavy artillery. These men, who made up the vast majority of the garrison at the numerous forts in general, received only the forage cap. The brass designating insignia issued for artillery consisted of crossed cannons, along with a company letter and regimental number. These were to be worn on the army dress hat, along with a red tassel and cord, a black ostrich plume, and a brass eagle device that looped up the left side of the brim. When only the cap was issued, the brass insignia was usually worn on top of the cap.

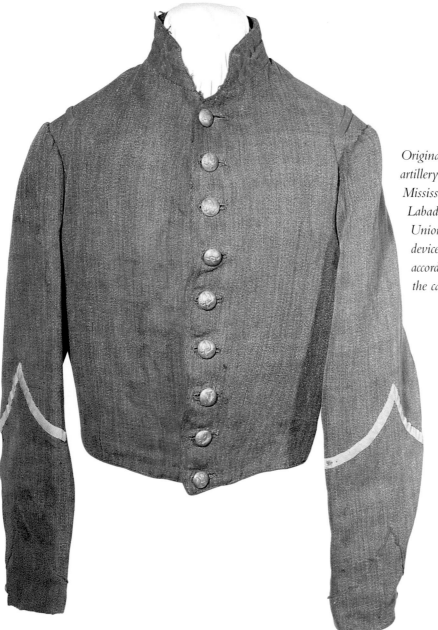

Originally a dark blue-gray jean cloth, this Confederate artilleryman's jacket belonged to a soldier of Battery H, 1st Mississippi, and was recovered from the battlefield of Labadieville, Louisiana, on October 27, 1862, by a Union soldier. The collar displays red cutout cannon devices, and the sleeves have yellow silk chevrons, which according to Mississippi regulations signify prior service in the cavalry. TROIANI COLLECTION.

Federal officer's regulation hat insignia for artillery, with metallic embroidered crossed cannons with the unit number against a red center. C. PAUL LOANE COLLECTION.

Coats and Blouses

The dress coat for the heavy artillery was cut the same as that for the infantry and was identical except for the trim on the collar and cuffs, which was artillery scarlet. Most heavy artillerymen also received the same fatigue blouse worn by other army enlisted men.

Trousers

Heavy artillery enlisted men wore the same trousers of sky blue kersey material issued to the infantry. The only difference was the color of the stripe, which designated a non-commissioned officer.

Shirts

Shirts were standardized in the army, and no distinction was made as to branch of service.

Other Items

During the time the men of the heavy artillery remained in garrison, life was measurably different than that of their comrades who served in the field with the light artillery or infantry. The personal belongings of a soldier of the 1st Maine Heavy Artillery who died on April 9, 1863, in the regimental hospital at Fort Alexander in the defenses of Washington, D.C., show a store of items that would be the envy of a combat soldier:[2]

1 Colt revolver and case	1 cap cover	1 thimble
1 bullet mold	1 drinking tube	1 neck tie
1 powder flask	1 knit jacket	1 testament [Bible]
1 box caps	2 woolen blankets	1 miniature [photograph]
1 wrench	1 knife and fork	1 pair boots
5 cartridges	1 tin plate	1 rubber blanket
13 postage stamps	6 steel pens	1 pair slippers
2 rings	1 comb	1 pair pants
4 pocket handkerchiefs	3 letters	1 cap
1 bunch letters	3 papers	1 dress coat
1 writing case	8 shirts	1 over coat
2 pen wipers	2 pair drawers	
9 skeins thread	3 pair socks	
2 bottles Jamaican Ginger	2 towels	
1 Nutty mixture	1 paper of pins	
1 pocket diary	2 papers of needles	

CONFEDERATE

As with the Union, the Confederate soldier serving as heavy artillery received nearly the same uniform as the infantry. Jackets seem to have been a common item of issue, along with caps. When trimmed, all uniform items of Confederate artillery issue would have received the traditional artillery scarlet.

LIGHT ARTILLERY

UNION

The guns served by the light artillery were taken into battle pulled by a six-horse team harnessed in pairs. Artillerymen serving as drivers rode mounted on the left horse in each team to control the quick movement of the gun into battle position. A battery of Federal artillery usually consisted of six guns of the same type, as well as the caissons and wagons needed to support the guns. The gunners for the foot artillery marched with the guns or rode on the ammunition chests. The horse artillery required all cannoneers to be mounted, a necessity to follow the rapid pace set by the cavalry they were supporting. The uniform of both branches of the light artillery more closely resembled those of the cavalry.

Headgear

Uniform regulations of 1861 called for the Federal light artillery soldier to be issued a cap with a scarlet horsehair plume, scarlet tassel and cord, and brass insignia that included an eagle and crossed cannons.[3] This cap closely resembled a shako, having a hard body that raised to 5 3/4 inches in front and 7 3/8 inches in the rear. It had a wide, stiff glazed visor, with the top, or crown, made of the same material. All in all, it was a handsome and very military-looking ensemble that was totally unsuitable for wear on anything but dress parade.

Some light artillery batteries were issued the M1858 army hat. Battery L, 2nd Illinois Light Artillery, received 140 "Artillery hats, complete" on April 5, 1862, with crossed cannons and an "L" and "2."[4] The battery is also listed with forage caps, but the hat apparently continued to be worn, as an order dated July 16, 1863, prohibited altering the shape of the hats.[5]

By far the most common headgear worn by the Federal light artillery was the M1858 forage cap, as shown in numerous requisitions and returns from volunteer batteries in every theater of the war, as well as numerous period photographs. An order issued to the light artillery at Camp Berry, Washington, D.C., on November 22, 1863, gave explicit instructions regarding the forage cap: "Hereafter every enlisted man of this post will wear the regulation forage cap, no caps of any other [type] will be worn by enlisted men either on or off duty, this order is not intended to prohibit noncommissioned officers from wearing caps of nicer material and manufacture provided they are of a pattern similar to the regulation Forage cap."[6]

Jackets and Blouses

Light artillery enlisted men, both volunteers and Regulars, were issued both a fatigue blouse and a waist-length jacket with a high-standing collar. The jacket, with its scarlet trim and twelve-button front, was a handsome uniform worn with great pride by most cannoneers. The men of the 6th New York Independent Battery were among many who had the jacket altered to give a more tailored appearance, often having the collar lowered at the same time. One man from the battery was detailed by the commanding officer as "company tailor." An order dated January 10, 1864, set the rate to alter a jacket at 50 cents.[7]

The four-button fatigue blouse for light artillery was identical to that issued to the infantry. The records of the 13th New York show that during 1863, they received ninety-one jackets and sixty-six blouses to replace those worn out in service or to uniform new recruits.[8]

Trousers

The light artillery received two types of trousers, both made of the regulation sky blue kersey material, due to the unique structure of the service that required both mounted and dismounted men. Cannoneers serving on foot received trousers that were identical to those received by the infantry. Mounted soldiers were issued trousers with an added layer of material in the seat and legs to compensate for the excessive wear caused by the saddle. A scarlet stripe designating a non-commissioned officer was worn as regulations dictated. An interesting order found in the records of Battery L, 1st Ohio Light Artillery, required all mounted men to "provide themselves with straps to hold down the legs of their trousers."[9]

Overcoats

Mounted Union artillerymen received overcoats identical to those worn by the cavalry, and those issued to foot artillerymen were identical to those worn by the infantry.

Footwear

Those serving in the light artillery received either boots, as issued to cavalry, or shoes, as received by the infantry, depending on whether they were mounted or dismounted.

Insignia and Accessories

The prescribed insignia for artillery, dating from 1836, consisted of brass crossed cannons along with the regimental number and company (battery) letter, universally worn on the hat or cap.[10] Light artillery batteries, designated independent batteries and not assigned to an artillery regiment, would wear only the number of the battery. These items were standard issue provided by the Quartermaster Department, although soldiers sometimes purchased and wore more ornate insignia.

Corps Badges

Beginning in the spring of 1863, the use of corps badges was mandated for all those serving within the ranks of the various army corps of the Army of the Potomac. Several corps within this army adopted a red, white, and blue variation of the prescribed badge for the headquarters staff. In several, this badge was authorized for the artillery attached to the corps, most notably within the I, III, and V Corps. Concerning the I Corps, Gen. Robert McAllister noted that "no special badge has been ordered for the artillery; but most of them have adopted the corps headquarters badge."[11]

The III Corps artillery's General Order No. 3, dated September 6, 1863, gave detailed drawings of a diamond-shaped badge to be worn by batteries attached to the three divisions of that corps. The badge was divided into four sections, each in the shape of a small diamond. Batteries assigned to the 1st Division had the upper and lower sections of red cloth, with the left section white and the right blue. The 2nd Division batteries wore the top and bottom sections white, with the left red and the right blue. The 3rd Division batteries had blue top and bottom sections, with the left red and the right white.[12]

At least two corps, the VI and the IX, simply ordered their artillery to wear the badge of that corps in scarlet or red. The order book of the 34th New York Independent Battery, which served with the IX Corps, contains an order dated April 10, 1864, calling for the use of the badge of that corps to be "worn on the top of the cap or front of the hat." Also acceptable was the use of a badge "of the same design, made of gold or gilt, silver or white metal, bronze or copper, to be attached to the left breast of the coat as a pin or suspended by a red, white and blue ribbon."[13] The following December 23, IX Corps General Order No. 49 in part restated the first order and, in addition, called for the men of the artillery brigade to wear the badge in red "under the regulation cross cannon."[14]

Shoulder Scales

During the decade preceding the Civil War, brass shoulder scales had been issued to all mounted troops. These scales were worn in the same manner as cloth epaulets, becoming universal with all branches of the army in 1855. During the war, many were issued to volunteers, but they were seldom worn. The issue and wearing of the scales within some volunteer batteries of light artillery are well documented. An order issued to Independent Battery C, Pennsylvania Light Artillery, April 13, 1864, states in part, "Shoulder scales and caps will be worn in all parades and duties when the jacket is required." The 24th New York Independent Battery received similar orders on July 22, 1863: "At retreat every man will appear in dress jacket and scales."[15]

CONFEDERATE

Confederate light artillery batteries were organized much the same as those in the Union army, with the exception that Confederate batteries often contained only four guns and frequently contained guns of mixed types. Unlike the Federal army, however, the Confederacy made no effort to provide a distinct style of uniform for the light artillery. It was only the color of the uniform trim, and in some cases that of the cap being worn, that set the artilleryman apart from the infantryman or cavalryman.

Headgear

The Confederate artillery enlisted man, like his comrades in the rest of the army, wore a variety of headgear. Hats were commonly issued with no description given, and the style was likely dependent upon what could be obtained at the time. Caps were issued in substantial quantity and in some cases were the most distinctive part of the Confederate artillery uniform. Regulations called for a cap with a red body, and such were indeed received and worn by some Confederate gunners. Examples exist that were worn by men in the 1st Battalion Virginia Light Artillery and Hart's South Carolina Battery.[16] On January 14, 1864, the Pee Dee Artillery of South Carolina received forty-five red caps. It is possible that these caps were a product of the Confederate quartermaster facility at Charleston, South Carolina.[17]

Jackets

The Confederate light artillery received uniforms from the same facilities that provided uniforms for the rest of the army. The issue of jackets was universal throughout the war. Until the last year of the conflict, many of those manufactured in Southern depots were trimmed in red or scarlet in the fashion adopted by that facility. The jackets imported under the Tait contract in 1864 were not trimmed.

Trousers

Confederate regulations called for the wearing of sky blue trousers by enlisted men, and it is likely that many were issued to the Confederate light artillery. It is equally likely that many were received courtesy of the Federal army via capture. As with the other branches of the Confederate army, the color and cloth of the trousers varied depending on availability, and gray or shades of brown were as likely to be part of any new issue received in the field. Unlike the Federal mounted soldiers, the Confederate artillerymen who rode into battle seldom, if ever, received trousers with the added layer of cloth reinforcement that was standard issue in the Union army.

Footwear

More often than not, the Confederate artilleryman, whether mounted or dismounted, received army-issue shoes. As with other items, these were exactly the same as those received by the infantry, and they suffered the same variances in quality as those worn by the foot soldiers.

Insignia

The Confederate Quartermaster Department made no issue of distinctive insignia, such as the crossed cannons commonly received by the Federal artillery. Chevrons and trouser stripes of scarlet were issued or fabricated in the field, and along with jacket trim, these served to distinguish the Confederate cannoneers.

Overcoats

Confederate overcoats were manufactured or imported in quantity but do not appear to have been produced or issued in distinct patterns for mounted versus dismounted troops, as in the Federal army. Some were made without capes, which were always present on those issued to Federal soldiers. Federal overcoats were prized items to the Confederate soldiers and were often worn by them, sometimes with unfortunate results resulting from mistaken identification as Yankees.

WASHINGTON ARTILLERY

In the decade prior to the outbreak of the war, the New Orleans newspapers carried numerous references to the city's premier and oldest militia organization, the Washington Artillery. Parades, rifle matches, and social functions seemed to be incomplete without members of the unit present. With their dark blue frock coats trimmed in artillery red, red kepis, white buff leather belts, and artillery sabers, the men of the Washington Artillery represented everyone's ideal of military men. Each man of the organization wore with pride the unique gold badge of the organization, crossed cannons surrounded by a belt with a gold tiger head suspended below. Upon the badge were engraved the words "Washington Artillery," along with a phrase that neatly summed up the spirit of the organization: "Try Us."

By 1861, the Washington Artillery was a battalion of four companies. On May 3, its commander, Maj. J. B. Walton, telegraphed the Confederate secretary of war stating that his battalion, numbering 300 men, was "ready and desirous to take the field." The service of the battalion was immediately accepted for the period of the war, and the men were ordered to report to Lynchburg, Virginia. From here they were ordered to Richmond and assigned to the Army of Northern Virginia. Shortly after the first battle at Manassas, the dress coats of the Washington Artillery were sent to Richmond to be used on "swell occasions," but the red kepis remained. During the next four years, the Yankees had ample opportunity to try the mettle of the men from New Orleans, which was never found wanting.

The Washington Artillery had the distinction of being represented in both theaters of the war. A fifth company was formed in New Orleans in February 1862. Rather than joining the rest of the battalion in Virginia, they made a name for themselves with the Army of Tennessee, seeing their first action at Shiloh on the morning of April 6, 1862.

DAVID RANKIN, JR.

Artillery officer's frock coat worn by Lt. Col. William Richardson Hunt as commander of the Briarfield Mississippi Arsenal from 1862 to 1865. As typical of many Confederate officers' coats, this fine specimen is outfitted throughout with Federal staff officers' buttons. GARY HENDERSHOTT.

Lieutenant Colonel Hunt's trousers, with a 1-inch-wide red woolen stripe on each leg. GARY HENDERSHOTT.

MCPHERSON'S RIDGE

Gettysburg, July 1, 1863: Two brigades of Union cavalry under the overall command of Brig. Gen. John Buford had taken position west and north of town and since early morning had been engaged with advancing Confederate infantry. Among the first to arrive to support the hard-pressed troopers was Lt. John Calef's Battery A, 2nd U.S. Artillery. The battery of six 3-inch rifle guns was met as it came onto the field by General Buford himself, dressed in an officer's sack coat and accompanied by a lone cavalry bugler. The general immediately ordered Calef to place his guns on either side of the Chambersburg Pike near the McPherson barn. Without hesitation, the battery moved forward, unlimbered, and went immediately into action.

The men of Calef's Battery, most of them proudly wearing the red-trimmed jackets of the Federal light artillery, were a familiar and welcome sight to the cavalrymen. The battery was entirely mounted and thus was able to accompany the fast-moving cavalry, giving them the extra firepower they needed. That firepower, added to the fast-firing carbines of the cavalry, enabled the troopers to hold this critical line until the Federal infantry of the I and XI Corps were able to relieve them.

Forage cap worn by Irish cannoneer Daniel P. Doyle of the 9th Massachusetts Battery between May 1864 and June 1865, when his unit served with the Reserve Artillery Brigade of the V Army Corps. The tricolored corps badge is unusual in that Doyle painted it directly on the crown of the cap. TROIANI COLLECTION.

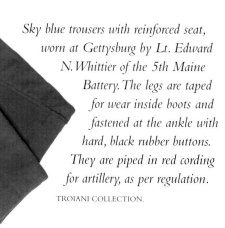

Sky blue trousers with reinforced seat, worn at Gettysburg by Lt. Edward N. Whittier of the 5th Maine Battery. The legs are taped for wear inside boots and fastened at the ankle with hard, black rubber buttons. They are piped in red cording for artillery, as per regulation.

TROIANI COLLECTION.

THE WATSON FLYING BATTERY, NEW ORLEANS, LOUISIANA, 1861

A New Orleans newspaper in July 1861 reported that the new Watson Flying Artillery was to be the finest company that has yet entered the field of Mars! Organized and equipped at an estimated cost of $40,000 to $60,000, the battery was raised and paid for by Augustus C. Watson, a wealthy planter and gambler from Tensas Parish, Louisiana. In its ranks were said to be the finest representatives of the old Creole families of New Orleans. Referred to as "men of wealth and high standings," they were proud to be garbed in the "resplendent uniforms" of Watson's Battery.

The battery's first captain was Allen Bursly, a West Point graduate touted in the papers as an experienced army officer. Bursly's first lieutenant, A. G. Gage, saw action during the Mexican War at the battle of Monterey. In a masterful coup, Watson was able to persuade Maj. Daniel Beltzhoover, chief of staff to General Twigg's Department of Alabama, Mississippi, and East Louisiana, to accept the position of battery commander. Beltzhoover was a West Point graduate as well, having served in the 1st Regiment of U.S. Artillery from 1847 to 1855. He also may have been attracted to the mystique of this rich man's company that was said to be "destined to attain a great celebrity in our [the Confederate] Army."

By the end of July 1861, the Watson Battery was complete. Four 6-pound bronze guns and two 12-pound howitzers mounted on "splendid gun carriages," with caissons and full appointments, were ready, cast and built in New Orleans by Edmund J. Ivers. Two hundred white horses, "the finest suited to the work in the State of Louisiana," would pull the guns.

At 4:00 P.M., on August 13, 1861, the men of the Watson Flying Artillery assembled in Lafayette Square. They were marched to the steamboat landing for the trip upriver to Augustus Watson's plantation. Their uniforms, equipment, horses, and guns would follow.

A very handsome uniform was chosen, with a nine-button shell jacket of steel gray, faced and piped in red crimson.

DAVID RANKIN, JR.

The jacket sleeves sported a French cuff, piped in yellow and adorned with eight ball buttons. The trousers were steel gray as well, with a red crimson stripe. The matching cap had a red cord, crossed cannons, and the brass letters "WB." The letters were purchased by battery members in honor of their founder, Augustus Watson. The black leather belt had a two-piece buckle bearing the Louisiana pelican state seal.

Equipped and staffed as it was, Watson's Flying Artillery should have had an envious record in the Civil War. Instead, the battery was destroyed not by Federal fire, but through internal dissension. Augustus Watson, in a patriotic gesture, enlisted in the company as a private, but to many he was a private in name only. The blue bloods of New Orleans felt

Bloodstained coat worn by Pvt. James Wiley Gibson, 1st South Carolina Artillery, when shot through the chest by a sniper while working on fortifications at Secessionville, South Carolina, on June 16, 1862. This plain seven-button frock coat was believed to be an example contracted by the state from Porter's Industrial School for Girls in Charleston. The piping was probably originally red.

COLLECTION OF THE CHARLESTON (SOUTH CAROLINA) MUSEUM.

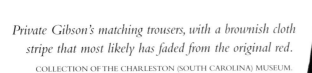

Private Gibson's matching trousers, with a brownish cloth stripe that most likely has faded from the original red.

COLLECTION OF THE CHARLESTON (SOUTH CAROLINA) MUSEUM.

that Beltzhoover drilled them too hard and seemed "rough and unfeeling." Arriving in Memphis on September 18, then ordered to Columbus, Kentucky, as part of the garrison, the Watson Battery began to break up. It was said that some members resigned to join the Louisiana Point Coupee Battery. A petition asking to be released from the battery and allowed to join some other unit was signed by forty of the men and sent to General Polk. With the situation unresolved, many of the men tore the "W" off their caps in protest of their dismal situation.

To make matters worse, in their first test under fire at the battle of Belmont, Missouri, on November 7, 1861, the entire battery of six guns was abandoned to the advancing Federals under U. S. Grant. Two of the guns were taken back to Cairo as trophies of war. Most of the battery horses were lost, forty-five killed outright in the battle, and all of the men's personal gear and tents were burned.

The battery continued to serve through the war until it was surrendered at Port Hudson, Louisiana, on July 9, 1863. This battery, once said to be destined for "celebrity in our Army," destroyed once at the battle of Belmont and again at the battle of Corinth, Mississippi, on October 3–4, 1862, left little in the way of records or documents to pass along their history. They were no doubt brave men, and in their "resplendent uniforms," they did indeed ride white horses into the halls of history.

2ND CONNECTICUT HEAVY ARTILLERY, 1864

The 2nd Connecticut Heavy Artillery shared a similar history and fate with several other regiments of heavy artillery that garrisoned the defenses of Washington in 1863 and early 1864. All of these regiments had been recruited as infantry, but upon reaching the nation's capital, helped build and then garrison the extensive system of earthwork forts that defended the city. Although the duty they were called upon to perform kept them out of harm's way, the constant drill as infantry as well as on the heavy guns mounted in the forts never let them forget they were soldiers.

Many of the 2nd Connecticut felt likely disappointment when they read of the battles and exploits of other regiments from their state. Had they been able to foresee the future, however, those who felt cheated serving as garrison soldiers perhaps would have had an appreciation for that mundane duty. As the summer campaign of 1864 began, the 2nd Connecticut and other garrison regiments were sent from the forts they occupied into the field, not as artillery but as infantry. Within the next year, most of these regiments more than made up for the months they spent in comparative security. The heavy artillery regiments wound up with more killed and mortally wounded in battle than any of the hundreds of infantry regiments that served in the campaigns of 1861–65. The 2nd Connecticut alone mustered out in August 1865 with a total of 12 officers and 242 men on its roll of honored dead.

The 2nd Connecticut had been originally raised as that state's 19th Infantry. It retained that regimental number until November 1863, when it officially became the 2nd Heavy Artillery. The change in designation also called for a change in uniform. Regimental Order No. 1, January 1, 1864, directed that all uniform jackets and hats be turned over to the regimental quartermaster, who would issue caps and dress coats. The order further stated that "no men . . . will be allowed to wear a hat of any kind."

Many of the troops in the Washington defenses received Enfield rifle muskets. While some turned them in and received Springfields before leaving the city, men of the 2nd Connecticut retained theirs. They would put them to good use in action from Spotsylvania to Appomattox as part of the famous VI Army Corps.

Note the exceptionally elegant tailoring and snug waistline. After serving with the 5th New York Volunteers, Duryée's Zouaves, and having been wounded at Gaines' Mill, Capt. Ralph E. Prime was commissioned lieutenant colonel of the 6th New York Heavy Artillery. TROIANI COLLECTION.

BATTERY LONGSTREET, BATTLE OF ANTIETAM, SEPTEMBER 17, 1862

DICK AND M. E. CLOW

For hours that must have seemed like an eternity, the Army of Northern Virginia held its own under relentless pounding by a Federal army determined to drive it from the field and back into Virginia. Casualties mounted by the minute on all quarters. Capt. M. B. Miller's 3rd Company of the famed Washington Artillery Battalion had sustained losses from Union sharpshooters, leaving him without enough cannoneers to serve all the guns in his battery.

Fully aware of the desperate conditions, Gen. James Longstreet seized the moment. Dismounting his staff to man one of Miller's Napoleon guns, and personally directing the fire, the Confederates fired double charges of case shot and canister into the ranks of Maj. Gen. Israel B. Richardson's Union Division, mortally wounding Richardson and seriously wounding Col. Francis Barlow, who commanded his right column. With their commanders down, the Federal attacks in this sector of the field slackened. The battle continued for several hours. For the Confederates, the timely arrival of reinforcements under Gen. A. P. Hill saved the day. Nowhere can the determination of the Confederates be better illustrated than here, with staff officers in full uniform manning guns to help fight a numerically superior Federal army to a standstill.

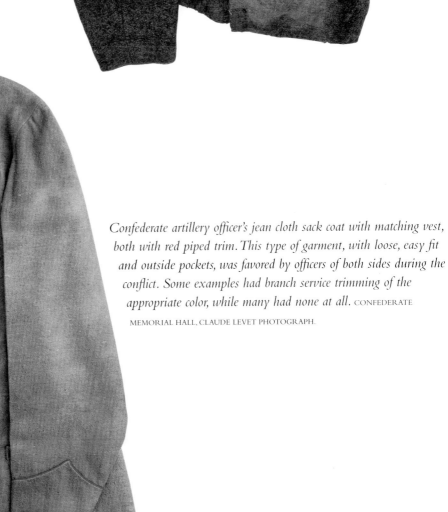

Richmond Depot type uniform jacket, worn by Lt. Daniel O. Merwin of Moody's Louisiana Battery when his right arm was shattered in a counterbattery duel at Garnett's Farm, Virginia, on June 28, 1862. This plain jacket has red piping and a gold cord rank bar on the collar. Surviving his wounds, Merwin was promoted to major and served at the camp of instruction at Enterprise, Mississippi, in 1863.
CONFEDERATE MEMORIAL HALL, CLAUDE LEVET PHOTOGRAPH.

Confederate artillery officer's jean cloth sack coat with matching vest, both with red piped trim. This type of garment, with loose, easy fit and outside pockets, was favored by officers of both sides during the conflict. Some examples had branch service trimming of the appropriate color, while many had none at all. CONFEDERATE MEMORIAL HALL, CLAUDE LEVET PHOTOGRAPH.

1ST COMPANY, RICHMOND HOWITZERS, 1863

VALMORE FORGETT

One of the better-known batteries of artillery to serve the Confederacy from the state of Virginia was the 1st Company of Richmond Howitzers. The company had its origin in 1859, and it was first called out in response to the perceived threat to the state following the John Brown raid on Harpers Ferry. At this time, the unit had been hastily equipped for the emergency and armed with muskets, with little in the way of uniform dress. As war clouds gathered, the company began a serious regimen of drill and ordered gray uniforms made. By the time it joined the Confederate army at Manassas, it had come a long way. Two other companies of

Richmond Howitzers were formed in May 1861, but the three never served together.

The corporal shown here leaning against one of the battery's howitzers is wearing the uniform that was typical of the Army of Northern Virginia in 1863. His jacket, which is piped in artillery red, is the second pattern produced by the Richmond Quartermaster Depot. His headgear is a cap, also trimmed in red for artillery. His boots are of fine quality and may have been of English origin, as is the belt visible under his jacket. The overcoat draped over the gun barrel came to him courtesy of the Yankees.

8th U.S. Colored Heavy Artillery, Private, Company K, 3rd Battalion, Late Summer 1864

This regiment was raised in Rhode Island during the last six months of 1863 as the 14th Rhode Island Heavy Artillery. Their designation was changed to the 8th U.S. on April 4, 1864, and to the 11th U.S. Colored Heavy Artillery in May of the same year. They continued to be carried on army rolls as the 8th Regiment until the fall, however.

Unlike many other colored regiments, the ranks of the 8th contained mostly men who had never known the yoke of slavery. Nearly all had been brought up free in their native state. An inspection report dated August 10, 1864, commented on the superior nature of the regiment and made special note of the fact that "the men are almost all free, and not freed men." It also noted that the majority of the regiment could read and write, and that the men were usually well informed. For such men to go and fight in the South took a special courage, as capture left open the possibility of a permanent loss of freedom.

Though it was heavy artillery, this regiment received the uniform jacket of the light artillery. As was the regulation with all regiments of heavy artillery, they received the arms and accoutrements of infantry. During the period before and after the Civil War, heavy artillery regiments drilled both on the large guns mounted in the various forts and as infantry.

The regiment was divided by battalions, with the 3rd Battalion serving its entire enlistment in the defenses of New Orleans. They were mustered out on October 2, 1865.

Federal artillery musician's uniform jacket, with a metallic gold thread edging in addition to the worsted regulation red piping. The original owner, William Henry Lewis of Battery G, 1st Rhode Island Light Artillery, undoubtedly felt the need for further ornamentation. An unexpected benefit of wearing a musician's heavily adorned jacket was articulated upon in a letter Lewis penned in June [1863?]: "I have got as pretty a Southeron damsel as ever you saw I went to here hous last night & had a good time there was a fiddel & other music I till you the read tape on my jacket draws gals rite to me." Bugler Lewis was mortally wounded at the battle of Cedar Creek, Virginia, in October 1864 and died shortly thereafter. COURTESY OF PAMPLIN HISTORICAL PARK AND THE NATIONAL MUSEUM OF THE CIVIL WAR SOLDIER.

WILLIAM HENRY LEWIS, UNPUBLISHED MANUSCRIPT, PAMPLIN PARK HISTORICAL PARK AND THE NATIONAL MUSEUM OF THE CIVIL WAR SOLDIER COLLECTION.

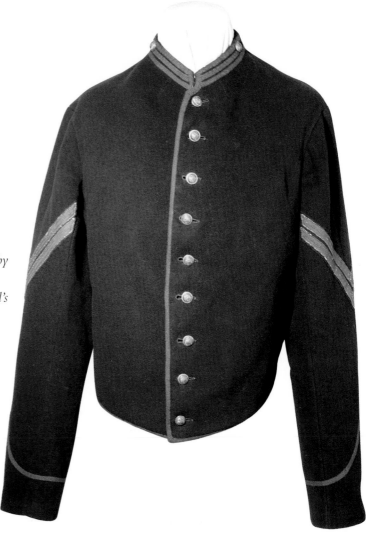

Uniform jacket of a New York artillery corporal. With a practical eye toward their own comfort, soldiers often modified regulation garments by lowering the collars and making various other changes. In many units, the officers turned a blind eye to such minor infractions, as this corporal's battery commander obviously did. Documents show instances where tailors were hired to customize jackets for entire units. TROIANI COLLECTION.

CRUTCHFIELD'S VIRGINIA, HEAVY ARTILLERY BATTALION

Like their counterparts in the Federal army, the Confederate soldiers who manned the heavy artillery batteries protecting their nation's capital spent most of their time drilling both as infantry and artillery. Serving in relative comfort, the heavy artillerymen perfected the skills of the soldier and waited. These men were described in glowing terms by Robert Stiles, who would later command them: "They were splendid soldiers in external appearance and bearing. I had never seen anything approximating to them in the field. Their dress parades, inspections, reports, salutes, bearing in the presence of officers and on guard, were wonderfully regular, accurate and according to the drill and regulations."

The true test of their soldiering ability did not come, however, until the final days of the war. With the collapse of the Petersburg line and the imminent evacuation of Richmond in April 1865, the heavy artillerymen under the command of Col. Stapleton Crutchfield spiked and abandoned their guns, and on April 2, they joined the retreating Confederate army. The men were now low on most supplies and were in light marching order. Many of the men were wearing Federal overcoats, which had served them well on duty in the defensive batteries. Now it was different. Maj. Robert Stiles warned them that in battle, the use of these coats could be dangerous. Despite this many opted for comfort over safety, with tragic results. At Sayler's Creek, Crutchfield's Brigade took up positions on the left of the Confederate line. In heavy fighting, Crutchfield was killed, and several of the men fell victim to fire from others in the brigade who, seeing the blue Yankee coats, mistook them for the enemy.

Rough gray wool enlisted man's frock coat, worn in the later part of the war by Sgt. Maj. Edward D. Robinson of Manly's Battalion, South Carolina Artillery. Dressed out with U.S. eagle buttons, it shows evidence of a sergeant major's chevrons (now missing) from Robinson's appointment to that rank in August 1864. This coat is similar to that described in the Confederate States' regulations for enlisted men. COLLECTION OF THE CHARLESTON (SOUTH CAROLINA) MUSEUM.

Regulation Federal-issue drum for artillery regiments. This example was made by C. & F. Soistman in Philadelphia, who in July 1864 had a contract for 100 three-quarter-size and 200 full-size artillery drums.

TROIANI COLLECTION.

E. J. COATES AND F. C. GAEDE, COMP., "U.S. ARMY QUARTERMASTER CONTRACTS, 1861–1865" (UNPUBLISHED MANUSCRIPT, 1993), 267.

CORPORAL, 4TH NEW JERSEY LIGHT ARTILLERY, DECEMBER 1864

TIM OSTERHELD

During the Civil War, U.S. Army uniforms were issued in only four sizes. This had been true before the conflict and would remain so for years afterward. Within the Regular army it was common practice for soldiers who took pride in their appearance to have the garments altered to create a more custom, tailored fit. During the war the practice was emulated by many serving as Volunteers. In some cases the practice resulted in condemnation by those in command. In others, however, it was condoned, with company or regimental tailors being designated to accommodate those wishing to enhance their military appearance. A few officers took personal pride in their units a step further by ordering certain changes in the uniforms. One of these was the captain of the 4th New Jersey Light Artillery Battery, George T. Woodbury.

The battery was organized at Trenton, New Jersey, and mustered on September 16, 1863. In February 1864 the following circular was issued to the Battery:

4th New Jersey Battery   Camp Berry, D.C.
                                February 26, 1864
   circular: The Captain Commanding has procured for the enlisted men red flannel linings for overcoats capes, at the price of $1.30 a piece. They will be put in by the Company tailor and the cost deducted from the pay of the men next pay day. The material is the same as that in the original coat furnished the Battery before leaving the state, having been procured from the firm who made the Company uniforms.
                                George T. Woodbury
                                4th N. J. Battery

Two months later Captain Woodbury's strict attention to detail within his command was further evidenced by his General Orders No. 1 issued at Gloucester Point, Virginia, on April 26 following the battery's assignment to the X Corps.

   The enlisted men of this command will immediately reduce their clothing to the following allowance; viz. 2 forage caps, 2 Artillery jackets, 2 pairs trousers, 2 pairs shoes or boots, 2 shirts, 2 pairs of drawers, 3 pairs of stockings, 1 blanket, 1 overcoat and 1 rubber blanket or gum overcoat. All clothing in excess of this allowance will be immediately packed, plainly marked and turned over to the QM Sgt.

Captain Woodbury resigned due to disability, and was succeeded by 1st Lt. Charles R. Doane. When corps badges were issued to the X Corps lieutenant (now captain) Doane, he maintained the exacting tradition set by his predecessor. On October 31, 1864, he issued General Order No. 17, which allowed no room for deviation.

   Corps Badges will be furnished on application to the QM Sgt. and every enlisted man is required to provide himself at once. The figure 4 will be placed below the cross cannon [on the cap] and the badge above with one of its points upwards and the opposite end directed toward the centre of the cross cannon. Care will be taken that the points are well stitched down.

The 4th New Jersey Battery was certainly one of the finest dressed of any group of cannoneers outside the Regular army. The unique scarlet-lined capes on their greatcoats predated the issue of such coats by the U.S. Army by at least fifteen years.

Sources

The Artillery

INTRODUCTION

1. Baron de Jomini, *The Art of War* (1838; reprint, Philadelphia: J. B. Lippincott, 1862).
2. National Archives, Record Group 94, Regimental Books, 1st Maine Heavy Artillery.
3. *Revised Regulations for the Army of the United States, 1861* (Philadelphia: George W. Childs, 1862).
4. Ibid., Battery L, 2nd Illinois Light Artillery.
5. Ibid.
6. Ibid., 1st Ohio Light Artillery.
7. Ibid., 6th New York Independent Battery.
8. Ibid., 13th New York Independent Battery.
9. Ibid., 1st Ohio Light Artillery.
10. Frederick P. Todd, *American Military Equipage, 1851–1872,* vol. 1 (Providence: Company of Military Historians, 1974).
11. James I. Robertson, Jr., ed., *The Civil War Letters of General Robert McAllister* (New Brunswick, N.J.: Rutgers University Press, 1965).
12. National Archives, Record Group 393, entry 214, III Corps Artillery Brigade Inventory and Inspection Reports.
13. Ibid., Record Group 94, Regimental Order Book, 34th New York Independent Battery.
14. *The War of the Rebellion: The Official Records of the Union and Confederate Armies,* vol. 42, (Washington, D.C.: Government Printing Office, 1901), part 3, 1066.
15. National Archives, Record Group 94, Regimental Order Book, 34th New York Independent Battery.
16. Editors of Time-Life Books, *Echoes of Glory* (Alexandria, Va.: Time-Life, 1991), Confederate vol., 163.
17. National Archives, Record Group 109, M-267, Compiled Service Records of Confederate Soldiers Who Served in Organizations from the State of South Carolina, Capt. Zimmerman's Company, Pee Dee Artillery.

WASHINGTON ARTILLERY

William Miller Owen, *In Camp and Battle with the Washington Artillery of New Orleans* (Boston: Ticknor, 1885), 49.

National Archives, Record Group 109, M-437, Letters Received by the Confederate States Secretary of War.

MCPHERSON'S RIDGE

The War of the Rebellion, Official Records of the Union and Confederate Armies, vol. 27 (Washington, D.C.: Government Printing Office, 1901) part 1, 1030.

Michael J. Winey, *Union Army Uniforms at Gettysburg* (Gettysburg, Pa.: Thomas Publications, 1998), 19–20.

THE WATSON FLYING BATTERY, NEW ORLEANS, LOUISIANA, 1861

New Orleans Daily Picayune, June 20 and August 12, 1861.

2ND CONNECTICUT HEAVY ARTILLERY, 1864

Frederick H. Dyer, *A Compendium of the War of the Rebellion* (New York: Thomas Yoseloff, 1959), 3:1007.

National Archives, Record Group 94, Regimental Papers, 2nd Connecticut Heavy Artillery.

BATTERY LONGSTREET, BATTLE OF ANTIETAM, SEPTEMBER 17, 1862

Stephen W. Sears, *Landscape Turned Red* (New York: Ticknor and Fields, 1983), 251.

1ST COMPANY, RICHMOND HOWITZERS, 1863

Lee A. Walker, Jr., *The Richmond Howitzers* (Lynchburg, Va.: H. E. Howard, 1993).

Editors of Time-Life Books, *Echoes of Glory* (Alexandria, Va.: Time-Life, 1991), Confederate vol., 135.

8TH U.S. COLORED HEAVY ARTILLERY, PRIVATE, COMPANY K, 3RD BATTALION, LATE SUMMER 1864

National Archives, Record Group 94, Regimental Books, 8th U.S. Colored Heavy Artillery.

Frederick H. Dyer, *A Compendium of the War of the Rebellion,* (New York: Thomas Yoseloff, 1959), 1722.

CRUTCHFIELD'S VIRGINIA, HEAVY ARTILLERY BATTALION

Robert Stiles, *Four Years under Marse Robert* (New York: Neale Publishing Co., 1910), 333.

CORPORAL, 4TH NEW JERSEY LIGHT ARTILLERY, DECEMBER 1864

Frederick H. Dyer, *A Compendium of the War of the Rebellion* (New York: Thomas Yoseloff, 1959), 3:1355.

National Archives, Record Group 94, Regimental Books New Jersey Light Artillery Batteries.